morality matters

morality matters

roger trigg

Blackwell
Publishing

BLACKWELL PUBLISHING
350 Main Street, Malden, MA 02148-5020, USA
108 Cowley Road, Oxford OX4 1JF, UK
550 Swanston Street, Carlton, Victoria 3053, Australia

First published 2005 by Blackwell Publishing Ltd

Library of Congress Cataloging-in-Publication Data
Trigg, Roger.
Morality matters / Roger Trigg.
p. cm.
Includes bibliographical references and index.
ISBN 0-631-23594-9 (hardcover : alk. paper) – ISBN 0-631-23595-7 (pbk. : alk. paper)
1. Ethics. 2. Political ethics. I. Title.

BJ1012.T74 2004
170–dc22
2003028153

A catalogue record for this title is available from the British Library.

Set in 10/12.5pt Dante
by Kolam Information Services, India
Printed and bound in the United Kingdom
by T J International Ltd, Padstow, Cornwall

The publisher's policy is to use permanent paper from mills that operate a sustainable
forestry policy, and which has been manufactured from pulp processed using acid-free
and elementary chlorine-free practices. Furthermore, the publisher ensures that the text
paper and cover board used have met acceptable environmental accreditation standards.

For further information on
Blackwell Publishing, visit our website:
http://www.blackwellpublishing.com

Contents

contents

Preface

This volume continues a long series of books I have written, taking a stand against various forms of relativism. My last book (*Philosophy Matters*, Blackwell 2002) argued that relativism ultimately undermines philosophy itself as an academic discipline. I now wish to look at alternatives to relativism in the controversial field of morality. I am also continuing my previous stress on the philosophical importance of the idea of a common human nature, forming the basis of societies which may at first sight appear very different.

The book took shape while I was visiting the Center of Theological Inquiry, a research institute in Princeton, New Jersey, for the latter part of 2002. The Center provided an ideal base for hard work and new inspiration. I am most grateful for the kindly hospitality I received there. I learnt much from colleagues visiting the Center from various parts of the world. I also received much stimulus from discussions in Princeton University, particularly at its Center for Human Values, and at the James Madison Program in American Ideals and Institutions.

I was very grateful for a research grant covering the same period, from the John Templeton Foundation. The Foundation furthers work in the area of science and religion, and, although the grant helped me primarily with other projects, it also indirectly aided this one.

As always I have enormously benefited from the help, support and encouragement of my family. My wife Julia, my daughter Dr Alison Teply and my son-in-law Robert Teply have all given invaluable advice and criticism.

Roger Trigg,
University of Warwick

Introduction

'That's Your Opinion'

A moral argument is often stopped in its tracks when someone refuses to consider a position by saying that 'that is just your opinion'. The implication is that anybody's judgement is as good as anyone else's, and that no one has a right to tell others what to do. The fact that I do not like bananas may be a fact about me, but it has no bearing on what you may enjoy. Similarly, it is implied, if I disapprove of something, that may tell you about me, but it has no relevance to what you should do. The confusion in all this is displayed by the idea that we have no 'right' to tell others what to do. We seem at the same moment to be denying that moral claims can tie everyone down, and asserting that there is at least one moral claim that we should all respect, namely that we ought not to impose our views on others.

How have we come to this point? We respect individual freedom, and consider that we are right to do so. Then, in the name of that freedom, many deny that morality can ever be other than a personal, even subjective, affair. What seems right to me is right for me, but not necessarily for others. This seems very tolerant, and we all value toleration. Yet the ideas of freedom and toleration are not morally neutral, but are only possible given a certain kind of society, which inculcates a definite moral position. A society in which toleration, and individual freedom, are only upheld in so far as they seem right to individuals is hardly one most of us would feel safe living in. Too much would depend on the passing whims, and tastes, of particular people. We would all want the reassurance of a more substantial moral framework, perhaps underpinned by the law of the land.

The confusion endemic in all this is well illustrated by those who want a right of individual 'privacy' to be publicly recognized. They then extend the idea of such privacy to cover wide-ranging personal judgements about our own preferred lifestyle. Privacy becomes 'autonomy', and 'autonomy' becomes the right to make my own choices without interference from others. Yet a right to such autonomy, whether claimed morally or enforced legally, involves a demand that others respect my own choices. Since very few choices fail to have public effects, this becomes a demand that I do what I like, regardless of its effect on others, and on the public good. In any social setting, such a position cannot be sustained. By claiming rights to privacy, we make other people's claims to similar rights unobtainable. We cannot all get what we want without colliding with others.

Morality cannot just be a matter of individual taste. Yet it is not just constituted by the customs and traditions of a particular society. We may want to criticize whole societies, including our own. In fact the same people who wanted to decry the idea of any universal morality, on the ground that it was merely an imposition of Western values, were the first to condemn apartheid in South Africa. If what is right is reduced to what is judged right in a particular society, white South Africa could claim to be a society. A common complaint was that 'you do not understand our circumstances, and would think differently if you lived here'. Yet if anything was objectively wrong, the apartheid regime, with its systematic racial discrimination, surely was. Otherwise, no one could properly condemn it. Yet condemnation had to appeal to basic moral principles that go deeper than the particular judgements of a particular society.

We have to be pulled back from a position that tolerates any and every view, including those that preach intolerance and hatred. No one can consistently use moral language, except in the most cynical way, without recognizing that it intrinsically makes judgements, calls on reasons which are applicable to everyone, and rules out some possibilities. Some philosophers, even so, have maintained that this truth-expressing function of moral language is wholly illusory. Saying that something is good, they would hold, only says something about ourselves, such as that we commend it. It is not making any claim about the world.

We see in these claims the long shadow cast by science. Its success in modern times has been such that it appears that truth has to be restricted to what can be decided according to its meticulous experimental method. It seems that truth cannot be at stake, if we have no agreed means of settling a dispute. This was the position of the 'logical positivists', who defined claims to truth in terms of our ability to verify or falsify them by scientific means. Thus claims, which cannot be checked, have no meaning. This view was propagated between the two world wars by the 'Vienna Circle', and it echoed through universities long after the Second World War. One of its main exponents in the English-speaking world was A. J. Ayer, whose book *Language, Truth and Logic* tried to show that moral statements were merely expressing emotion, evincing one's own feelings and perhaps calculated to stir those of others. Moral statements were 'emotive', not saying anything. Ayer claimed that 'it is impossible to find a criterion for determining the validity of ethical judgements, because they have none'.[1] Sentences expressing moral judgements are not able to express truths or falsehoods. They do not say anything at all.

This view resonated through society long after logical positivism was discredited as a philosophical theory. The idea remains strong that 'facts' are the province of science, while moral judgements are to be contrasted as 'values'. Facts are objective, and 'values' personal. To say that something is a 'value judgement' then becomes an effective device for stopping a conversation. The idea is that no reason can be given for what appears an arbitrary subjective choice. This is reinforced by the dominant idea that, as it is fallacious to deduce a value judgement from any particular set of facts, there is no rational way of passing from a particular circumstance to a judgement of what ought to be done. It seems that our personal choices must not be constrained by whatever happens in the world.

The issue is whether moral judgements can be made rationally, and should be influenced by anything outside our own arbitrary will. Can they be open to discussion and argument? Otherwise moral beliefs become mere facts about individuals or groups. Some have some preferences, or desires, while others have different ones. The temptation in a democratic society will be to count heads, or to conduct sociological surveys, to gauge what people think. Morality becomes a matter of opinion polls. What becomes important is simply meeting as many people's wishes, or failing to offend as many, as possible. The opinions are basic data, so that the question is no longer who is right, but how many believe something. It is irrelevant why they believe it. Morality then becomes politics. Moral issues become the stuff of political negotiation. We are only concerned with what can obtain maximum agreement. Moral argument is squeezed out of the public sphere, to be replaced by political compromises. Any idea of principled reasoning is abandoned in favour of negotiations and accommodations between interest groups.

This is precisely what is happening in many democratic countries, particularly when they are faced with basic disagreements. So-called 'pluralist' societies with many different beliefs coexisting alongside each other may find this strategy a tempting way out of seemingly endless arguments. They can avoid moral questions and concentrate on the toleration of difference and diversity. Instead of resolving disagreements, they may hope to find a way of steering through them. The idea of law as based on a moral vision is regarded as illiberal and intolerant, and involves siding with some interest group against another. Yet the contradictions in all this are glaring. We may uphold tolerance because we believe we should not stand for one moral vision rather than another, but the idea of a tolerant society, protecting individual freedom, is as substantive a moral position as one could wish. In fact, it would still be repudiated in many countries. The ideal of total moral neutrality must always be an illusion, since it itself embodies a view of what a good society should value most.

A Just Society?

We cannot escape moral choices. The only question is on what basis they are made. Democratic negotiation may appear to be a way of avoiding irresolvable issues. In a democracy, however, majorities win, and minorities lose. One of the most influential of modern political philosophers, John Rawls, attempted to meet this problem by envisaging social cooperation as taking place under a framework agreed by citizens, before they know their own place in the society. He put forward what he termed 'the idea of the original position', which envisaged a hypothetical social contract, according to which agreements are made under what he called a 'veil of ignorance'. The parties to the agreement have to establish a society of free and equal citizens, but they do not know their own position in the society, or what particular beliefs they might hold. The point is to specify basic rights and liberties, by eliminating what Rawls calls 'the bargaining advantages that inevitably arise within the background institutions of any society from cumulative social, historical and natural tendencies'.[2] There has to be an agreement on the principles regulating a society, without anyone having any inbuilt advantage or prejudice. No one knows whether they are going to be in a majority or minority, and, if persecution were to be allowed, they do not, according to this picture, know if they would be among the persecuted. The assumption is that this device of representation of a contract shows that justice involves not taking sides, because we do not know which side we would be on. Such an idea is driven by ideas of advantage. We want to do, it seems, what is best for ourselves. The snag is that we do not know what will achieve this, and so, for our own protection, have to take up a position advocating fair treatment for all.

This is a powerful picture, but the idea of justice being purveyed is inevitably political, arising from negotiation and agreement. Even so, it is clearly influenced by the preconception that all citizens are free and equal, and that they should cooperate. I should not, it seems, be able to indulge my own desires without respecting those of other people. Rawls's solution is, as he admits, an alternative to other possible answers. He asks, for instance, whether the terms for cooperation might 'be recognized by these persons to be fair by reference to their knowledge of an independent moral order'.[3] As an example, he asks if they are to be recognized 'as required by natural law'. Rawls has no patience with that kind of view, and his generation of justice from ideas of hypothetical personal advantage depends on stripping each person behind the veil of ignorance of everything that gives them individuality.

Is the fact that we belong to a particular country, or even are members of families, of no moral relevance? Is it wrong for us to favour our compatriots or own children? Does 'fairness' flatten out all distinctions between people? An ethic might be thereby generated which not only seems devoid of human feeling, but seems to challenge it. Patriotism becomes something of which to be ashamed. Love of family becomes classed as nepotism. All this seems to go against the grain of human nature. We want to belong. We want to love our children. We may want to be loyal to our country. Are such impulses to be controlled in the interests of a cosmopolitan law, stressing our global responsibilities?

Reference to human nature suggests that we can never realistically leave it behind, and still be ourselves. Humans have desires and needs, which very often stem from a common humanity which we all share. This itself may give a powerful motive for seeing all humans as free and equal. Every time the idea of human rights is invoked, the implication is that being human matters. Those who uphold the idea of human rights, while simultaneously denigrating the idea of humanity, are going to have a hard time. They will have to explain who possesses such rights. Yet such rights carry even wider implications. They are often invoked in contemporary moral and political rhetoric, but it looks, at least at first sight, as if the whole notion depends precisely on the kind of independent moral order which Rawls dismissed.

The idea of any moral order was decried by philosophers whose ideas of truth, and verification, were conditioned by science. It can look like meaningless metaphysics. Yet part of what theorists about a natural law in ethics have maintained is that our interests as human beings are closely linked with what is natural. We may go against the grain of nature, but we do so at a cost. Unless the idea of any human nature is totally ruled out, we should not be surprised that some things are good for us and others not. We are free to make wrong choices, but we cannot avoid the harm that they inevitably bring. Eating the wrong kind of food, or not having the right amount, will make us unhealthy. Similarly, different arrangements in society may well have different effects on how we flourish, both individually and collectively. A society encouraging policies which produce a major reduction in the birth rate will find it progressively harder to support an ageing population. Its future is in jeopardy if it cannot replace its population. A combination of many individual and 'private' choices will have produced a situation in which a whole way of life is at risk. People's actions always have wider consequences than they often realize, or intend. We cannot cherish our autonomy to the extent of believing that we have no contribution to make to the kind of society we live in.

The controversial area of marriage provides a good example. A decision as to whether to marry or remain single is one of our most cherished individual rights. This, if anything does, provides an example of where individual freedom is vital and has to be protected. Yet many extend this idea and regard it as an assault on their individual freedom that they cannot personally redefine what marriage is. Do they have to go through a public ceremony to have a relationship recognized? Should long-term partners be treated in the same way as husbands and wives? How long, anyway, is 'long-term'? Can same-sex relationships count as marriage? Whatever the answers to these questions, they involve major questions of public policy, even involving taxation, and concern the kind of society we live in. As such, they cannot be left haphazardly to individual choice. The private and the public cannot be so easily separated. Those who demand absolute personal freedom simultaneously want public recognition of their choices. A public debate cannot be avoided, and that has to involve moral questions about our priorities in society. It is not a simple political matter of what agreement can be obtained, or compromises extracted.

Should Law Enforce Morality?

The problem of the relation of individual freedom, morality and public policy was dramatized in the Opinion of the United States Supreme Court in the case *Lawrence* v. *Texas* in 2003. The case involved extremely controversial questions about the criminality, in Texas, of homosexual practices, but the matter was widened so as to have implications for the enforcement of any 'moral' view. The question is how far public law should be concerned with the enforcement of a particular morality, in this instance one concerned with sexual practices. The Opinion of the Court, which was not unanimous, argued with reference to moral principles that 'the issue is whether the majority may use the power of the State to enforce these views on the whole society through the operation of the criminal law'.[4] Quoting from a previous judgment in 1992, they claim that 'our obligation is to define the liberty of all, not to mandate our own moral code'. The Court thus puts the weight of United States law behind preserving liberty. That is all very fine, but it is disingenuous to pretend that the maintenance and preservation of individual liberty is not itself an important moral principle, particularly when it is none too clear what is meant by individual liberty.

The Court appears to be championing one moral position against others. There may be very good reasons why the law should not try to interfere with what goes on between consenting adults, literally in private, behind closed doors. The Court in its Opinion, however, goes far beyond the particular circumstances of this one case. The question of privacy becomes a much wider doctrine. The Court admits that it is giving voice to a changed, and extended, understanding of the nature of liberty, referring to what it calls 'an emerging awareness that liberty gives substantial protection to adult persons in deciding how to conduct their private lives in matters pertaining to sex'.[5] Thus a narrow idea of privacy becomes widened into a doctrine of autonomy over one's personal life, irrespective of any public effects. Whether one agrees with it or not, one cannot pretend that the Court is being morally neutral about the kind of society it is trying to achieve. One of its members, Justice Scalia, in a dissenting opinion, claims that 'it is clear that the Court has taken sides in the culture war, departing from its role of assuring, as neutral observer, that the democratic rules of engagement are observed'.[6] In his view, substantive questions ought to be settled democratically, not 'imposed by a governing caste that knows best'.

If the law stands back from individual moral decisions, whether about sex or anything else, on the ground that they are 'private', this certainly seems consonant with a liberal respect for liberty. It is, however, illusory to suppose that that this is not itself a substantive moral decision, with good or bad consequences for society. As such, there is then the related question of whether courts are the appropriate instruments in a democratic society for making these decisions. This is not just an American problem. With the introduction of legislation upholding human rights in the European Union and elsewhere, it is now common in many countries for courts to make rulings against legislation, even though it had been democratically agreed. Laws have to meet certain standards, which are defined by judges. This reinforces the question as to the basis of human rights, and whether judges have special insights into their nature, which are denied the rest of us. Such matters extend far beyond the controversial areas of sexual morality. It becomes very difficult to view the law as a neutral referee when it is playing such a major role in shaping our various societies.

The stress on individual liberty and autonomy goes with a very individualist approach to society. We may all agree on the intrinsic importance of the individual, though even that agreement should not be taken for granted. It is still different from thinking that society is just the by-product of the interaction of individuals. We all need each other. Aristotle's idea that humans are political animals stresses that we come together in society because it is in our nature to do so, and not just because it is advantageous for us. The idea that we are all members of a wider whole is part of what lies behind the traditional emphasis on natural law, stemming from Aristotle. This does not suggest that we are conditioned so as to act in one way rather than another. It has traditionally suggested that we can use our rationality to understand how we can fulfil our own nature as human beings, or go against it. The assumption is that we will flourish if we act in accordance with our true nature. We are free to go against it, but if we do so, there will be inevitable costs.

Unlike physical laws about gravity or suchlike, natural law tells us what ought to happen, not what will happen. It has often been thought that it provides a suitable yardstick against which the laws of a country can be measured. It provides a moral basis for positive law, and is thus a very different position from the idea that law should not take sides in moral disputes. Aristotle certainly did not think that the law simply provided the rules according to which people of different beliefs could live together. For him, politics was bound up with morality. He thought that the role of law was to help us to live moral lives for own good and for that of the community. Law should teach us good habits so that what we begin by doing because instructed by the law, we finally do because it has become part of our character. Law educates.

This idea of the law as teacher is linked with the view that human beings have definite characteristics. If our choices of lifestyle carried no particular consequences for ourselves, or for others, autonomy might be more attractive as the supreme moral principle. If, though, we cannot mould the needs of our nature to meet our preferences, morality will need to have some content if it is to guide us in living fulfilled lives. Some might wish we could live our lives like artists facing a blank canvas, so that we can express ourselves, as we wish, in a burst of total creativity. If, though, we cannot change human nature, we may find that such freedom only produces disaster.

It is hardly surprising that the idea of any fixed, or shared, human nature is denied in some quarters. Despite recent neo-Darwinian theories stressing the importance of our genetic constitution, so-called 'postmodernists' continue to resist the notion of any nature common to us all, which underlies apparent differences between societies and traditions. Richard Rorty, for example, has argued against the idea of 'nature' at all levels. He writes that 'since nothing has an intrinsic nature, neither do human beings'.[7] Yet he still cannot resist referring to 'humans' and talking of the need to work for what he terms a 'better human future',[8] while rejecting the notions of 'reality', 'reason' and 'nature'. Yet without these ideas, the problem remains of what a better future for humans could possibly be. We cannot use our reason, it seems, to see what is good for humans, and we have no nature against which judgements about what is better for us can be judged. Perhaps we just have to agree what we want. Yet when we get it, we may be horrified, because, after all, it does not meet human needs.

Rorty, like many others, wants to use fashionable platitudes about human rights without invoking humanity. He says: 'To speak of human rights is to explain our actions by identifying ourselves with a community of like-minded persons – those who find it natural to act in a certain way.'[9] Yet the whole point of talking of rights is to claim that they apply even in communities of those who are very unlike us. Rights are universal, or they are nothing. Rorty's use of the word 'natural' in this context is particularly odd, since he certainly does not believe in 'nature'. Indeed, the implication is that what some people find natural, others will not. That inverts the very idea of nature.

Some of the most vexed political questions of the present time – human rights, the function of law, the relevance of human nature and human claims to be free and equal – are all linked. Without the idea of a shared human nature, we may well be able to forget the rest of the world and retreat into the cocoon of a community of 'like-minded persons'. We can be complacent in our agreements, without questioning their basis, or worrying why others do not share our views. Morality can be relegated to a matter of personal taste, or of social convention. Yet if that happens, as Plato saw, with his discussion of justice at the start of the *Republic*, justice will become whatever the powerful want it to be.

The alternative to a rational morality claiming a universal applicability has always been control by the powerful, whether that means the wealthy, those able to use the most force or simply those in the majority. Without the rule of law, resting on a moral foundation, bare power will always win. Morality matters, not just because it should govern our personal behaviour and the way we treat others. It should provide the context in which all affairs are conducted, and nations governed. Morality can never be the product of individual whim, or passing fashion. It is the indispensable foundation for any properly ordered society.

Notes

1   A. J. Ayer, *Language, Truth and Logic*, Victor Gollancz, London, 1946, p. 108.
2   John Rawls, *Political Liberalism*, Columbia University Press, New York, 1993, p. 23.
3   Ibid., p. 22.
4   *Lawrence v. Texas*, 539 US 558, 123 S.Ct 2472, 2480, 156 L.Ed.2d 508 (2003).
5   *Lawrence*, at 2480.
6   *Lawrence*, at 2497 (Scalia J., dissenting)
7   Richard Rorty, *Philosophy and Social Hope*, Penguin Books, London, 1999, p. 63.
8   Ibid., p. 27.
9   Ibid., p. 85.

1

What is natural?

Is Morality Natural?

Many nowadays, in their pursuit of self-interest, are cynical about the point of morality. They do not think it matters, and are none too clear about what it is really about. When Plato said, at the beginning of the *Republic*, that justice is merely 'the interest of the stronger', he was himself convinced that this was far from the truth. For him, morality was a matter not of who could get their own way, but of conforming to ethical standards, such as justice and goodness, that exist totally apart from humans. They have a claim on us, but we do not create them. They are there, more real, Plato thought, than even the ordinary material world around us.

Many would be far from convinced if morality was severed from anything to do with human beings. The other extreme is to think that it is merely a matter of what we want to do. Yet we each want different things, and many of them conflict. No one can have all their desires satisfied. In addition, if we get what we want, it very often is not good for us. Our wants are very often far apart from what we need, or from what it is in our interest to have. Our short-term desires, say for rich food, may too often be at odds with our long-term ones, say to be healthy.

Desires on their own are not a very good guide to action. If we each act on immediate impulse, the result will soon be disastrous, both for ourselves and for others. That still does not fully explain why we should take as much notice of other people as of ourselves. It does not help us, either, to understand what is good for ourselves. Do we start with the mere fact of what we naturally want, or is there some other standard? What role does human nature play in morality? There are two issues here, both how far human nature itself can be a source of our moral impulses such as sympathy for others, and how far it provides the raw material for our moral judgements. If, after all, we do not understand what we need as humans, we are hardly in a position to help each other.

Certainly morality is not content to accept what actually happens, and the way people actually behave. It is 'normative' in the sense that it sets standards for what we ought to do. Human nature is inherently ambiguous, in that it can be a source of impulses that morality has to control, as well as ones that can be fostered. There are moral claims on us, it appears, even when we do not recognize them. Yet what is their source? One way in which humans appear to be distinct from animals and the rest of nature is precisely their ability to see their faults, and make decisions about what they ought to do. They can see alternatives and choose between them. Some would claim that we have some form of moral sense, which enables us to react indignantly to injustice, and to sympathize with those in trouble. Others would see morality as the mere product of social arrangements. Both views suggest that humans are detached from the natural world. This, though, makes us confront the question of the relation of morality to what is natural.

What Does 'Being Natural' Mean?

In the midst of current controversies about genetic engineering, and biotechnology, it is often easy to react against some new procedure or other on the grounds that it is 'unnatural'. Something in us makes us shrink instinctively from implanting the genes of one species into another, or from letting people have clones of themselves produced. Yet human clones already exist 'naturally' in the shape of identical twins. Similarly, cuttings of plants have produced 'clones' for generations of gardeners. Our misgivings, though, still remain.

Our reactions to what is 'natural' may in fact sometimes be merely a matter of what we are accustomed to. It would be hard to suggest that it is any more natural to drive on the left rather than the right side of the road. It is possible that, for right-handed people, it might be more natural to defend oneself with a sword, with one's right hand, and keep one's left side from being exposed. That might be a historical reason for why people went on the left. This, though, only raises further questions. A left-handed person might find it better to go on the right, and so there might be a minority preference for that. A rule of the road could not claim any validity, without there being an agreement as to what everyone should do. Even then it would not be universal, but only extend as far as the agreement. We are, in other words, in the realm of convention, of an agreement that could be formulated in different ways. This is different from what is natural. What always or generally happens is different from what depends on some agreement for its occurrence.

Another issue is how far what is 'natural' merely refers to what does happen, or whether it has a normative element. What would follow from an observation that people tend to go the left (or right) if given a free choice? It may seem as if what generally happens is not very relevant to what ought to happen. A reasonable conclusion may be that it does not matter in the slightest which side of a road one goes on, as long as everyone in a particular area agrees to do the same. The country that is said to have decided to change from driving on the left to the right, but to phase in the change gradually, was not pursuing a viable policy.

Is all behaviour to be regarded, like rules of the road, as a matter of convention? We all have to live together, and we have to agree to behave in ways that, in reality or metaphorically, do not make us collide with one another. Many find it difficult to accept that the rules by which we live, and which govern our relations with others, are purely arbitrary. Are they just the result of political negotiation and agreement? In that case, where did the original beliefs and preferences of the negotiators come from? Are all our inclinations and desires to be regarded as random? It may be difficult to imagine the hypothetical picture of those involved in arriving at some original agreement or contract. What is much clearer is that when we have been brought up in a particular context, it is easy to take what always happens as 'natural' when it may have a purely local, parochial, significance. To take the example of driving again, it is easy in a new country, driving on the 'wrong' side of the road, to feel that one is in a 'looking-glass' world where everything happens in an inverted way. It seems in the highest degree 'unnatural'. Yet as one will get that feeling driving on either side of the road, if it is a different one from one's upbringing, this has everything to do with custom, and little to do with what the world is actually like.

What seems unnatural may be little more than what is unfamiliar. This underlines the fact that appeals to nature may not have much to do with the character of the world. Furthermore, they may carry no ethical import. Something does not have to happen just because it usually does. Indeed, even if we do find that the world does work in a particular way, why should that govern our actions? Buried deep in the heart of modern moral philosophy lies the injunction that one should never attempt to derive an 'ought' from an 'is'. Just because something does happen does not mean that it ought to. 'Facts' and 'values' are logically different. Deriving ethical statements from those about the world is an example of the so-called 'naturalistic fallacy'. All of these injunctions, which are closely related, suggest that nature – or what does happen – can never give us ethical guidance. The world (whatever that may be) is morally neutral. We, as humans, have to pick what is relevant for our own interests. Is, though, such a decision to be an arbitrary choice, or is our decision to be grounded in what we naturally need or want?

It is very easy to see familiar customs as grounded in the way the world is, even though they may be accidental, or only loosely related to facts in the world. They could just as well have been otherwise without any notable effects. The word 'natural' is in fact a slippery one, and philosophers have long been wary of it. In the eighteenth century, David Hume said of the definition of the word 'nature' that 'there is none more ambiguous and equivocal'.[1] One distinction is that between the natural and the supernatural. Hume was himself disposed to distinguish between miracles and all other events (with the possible implication that miracles did not really occur). This means that all ordinary events are 'natural', and that if a miracle did take place, perhaps it would thereby have to be classified as a natural event. If 'nature' simply encompasses everything that happens, the contrast with the supernatural becomes simply that between what can and does happen, and what cannot and does not. Ruling out anything supernatural can be just another way of stating a materialist position, according to which physical events comprise reality.

The concept of natural law is as ambiguous as any other use of the term 'natural'. Is the term simply an invocation of fixed laws of nature, governing the way the world works? In that case, as Hume indicates, nothing can really go against such a law. If it happens, it has to be natural. As well as the opposition between the natural and the supernatural, Hume also points out two other contrasts. The first is with the rare and the unusual, although he is the first to admit that this offers a very imprecise standard. His assumption is not that something cannot happen because it goes against nature, but that it is unusual for it to occur. The converse is that the natural is what is usual. It could be said that hunger is the natural state of humanity, even if we now have the power (if not always the will) to go against nature. Here all that is meant is the unfortunate fact of the prevalence of hunger in the world. From another point of view, indeed, one could say that hunger is profoundly unnatural, in that it is a part of our nature to eat so as to stop being hungry. It may even seem as if there is something wrong with being hungry. In that case, the concept of nature becomes ethically relevant. Other things being equal, it may seem that people ought to have their natural desires met. Being hungry or thirsty is a good reason for being given food or drink. This, though, is to step from what is the case to what ought to be, and that is always a contentious step.

Hume's second contrast is between nature and the artificial. Most of what we term 'nature', the farmed countryside and the preserved wilderness, is, in this sense, artificial. It is the product of human intervention. Fields and woodlands, even the cleared moorland, all bear the marks of centuries of cultivation. Nothing bears witness to this more than the carefully contrived 'natural' look of planted woods and new lakes produced by eighteenth-century landscape gardeners, such as 'Capability' Brown in England. The ancient trees and sinuous lakes may provide charming vistas, and apparently have been there since time immemorial. They are the result of human contrivance, and not an accident of nature. Even the trees and plants themselves have often been the result of human selection and propagation.

Hume uses his distinctions to ask if human virtue is natural or not. Since it is not supernatural, it is natural according to his first distinction. Yet if the standard is what is usual, it may be, as Hume cynically points out, that virtue is highly unnatural. As to his third distinction, he assumes that virtue and vice are both the result of artifice and not nature. Yet is this all that can be said about our moral connections with the world? Hume himself was the major proponent of the position that passing from what is the case to what ought to be the case is simply fallacious. Facts for him were empirically checkable, and all else in this realm became a matter of human psychology. Our reactions to events may be predictable and intelligible because of our knowledge of human nature. They could not be justified by the character of the events themselves. The 'natural' could not ground our ethical judgements. Events and our reactions to them are distinct. Hume could not allow that 'nature', however defined, could give any rational justification for the way we behave. Our passions and emotions are not subject to reason. As he famously claimed, reason was the slave of the passions. We may therefore naturally feel sympathy, but we could never be told that we ought to be sympathetic in any given situation.

When natural law is talked about, it is not just the definition of the term 'natural' that is difficult, but also the question of whether those laws are fixed. The physical laws of nature are not prescriptive. They do not command what has to happen, but describe what does. Water normally boils at 100 degrees Celsius, but that does not mean that it ought to. There is nothing 'wrong' with water not boiling at that temperature, and it will not do so at altitude. 'Nature' in this context is just what tends to happen in normal circumstances. Many want to see nature as more than this. They want to view nature as a guide as to what ought to happen. Yet a view that natural law governs the world in some prescriptive manner can be thoroughly determinist, suggesting that the events of the world unfold in an inexorable pattern of cause and effect. Each happening can be explained wholly in terms of the nexus of events that had previously occurred. Modern physics suggests that the old idea of the universe as a piece of clockwork, much in vogue in the eighteenth century, is inadequate. The indeterminism of quantum mechanics is particularly relevant in showing how, at least at the most fundamental level, any simple model of cause and effect breaks down. Matters are even more clear-cut when our ability to predict events is brought into question. Chaos theory shows how infinitesimal differences can have large effects, even though we may not be able initially to detect them. The result has to be a limit in principle to predictability by humans. Some parts of the workings of nature will be impossible for us to grasp completely, including such ordinary things as very detailed predictions of weather.

This fact alone must make us cautious in using 'nature' as an absolute guide for human action. The more human knowledge increases, the more we become aware of limits on our knowledge. We cannot escape the fact of human freedom, and coupled with that, of our fallibility. The picture of a predetermined world, unfolding in a predictable manner, according to laws ordained by the Creator (or developed through evolution), has to be deeply flawed. In the past, much effort has been expended, in reflections on human morality, over the question of whether we can make a difference to the world, or whether everything, including our own decisions, and actions, are merely the effect of previous causes, possibly physical. The material world may have its regularities, but it is neither wholly predictable by humans nor wholly caused to develop or change in particular ways.

The demise of physical determinism makes human freedom, and the responsibility we bear for our choices, of central importance. Our freedom is not an illusion. Yet on what basis can we, and should we, make our decisions? Much is made of the alleged difference between events in the world and the value humans happen to place on them. The idea is that ethical weight is placed on the decision, rather than on any grounds for it. In other words, morality is solely a product of human judgement and has nothing to do with intrinsic characteristics of the world. The latter are ethically neutral, and it seems that it is up to humans to impose any meaning or value on them, in the light of their interests, needs and desires. A long series of distinctions in moral philosophy have held that facts are logically distinct from values, that what is the case is wholly different from what ought to be the case or that a description is of a different kind from evaluation. The conclusion of each position is the same, namely that what goes on in the world cannot give any rational guidance about what ought to happen. The world and our moral decisions are thus insulated from each other. By definition, 'nature' should then offer no prompting as to what we ought to do.

We have a freedom to act and we are not a part of any rigid mechanism. The freedom, though, does not seem to be grounded in the way things are. It appears to involve a decision made in a vacuum. Indeed, many philosophers have concluded that facts are objective, and a part of the furniture of the world. They are established by science. Values, on the contrary, are subjective, and the result of human decisions. They cannot be grounded in anything beyond themselves, and are ultimately not bound by reason. They are random or, at best, the result of arbitrary human agreement.

The result of this dichotomy is to cast 'values' adrift. So-called 'value judgements' are made to be personal matters of opinion, as opposed to checkable matters of fact. They become merely what people happen to value at a given time or place. They seem to tell us more about those who do the valuing than about what is being valued. Many then see moral disagreement as a clash between people, to be resolved by political means. It is not a disagreement about the way things are, in which one side is right and the other mistaken. In science, no one would ordinarily see a disagreement as a mere matter for political negotiation. Compromise may help people to live together but it does not necessarily produce truth. The world (or 'reality') should also have a say. Yet morality is in many people's eyes very different.

Our moral decisions are made to look as if they need have nothing to do with the way things are. 'Nature' seems not to enter into our moral calculations. Sociology, or psychology, sometimes claims to be able to tell us more about why people adopt the moral positions they do. There is certainly a story to be told about human ethical reactions. Human sociobiology and evolutionary psychology try to show the roots of our moral reactions.[2] Both use neo-Darwinian theory to explain how we come to be moral beings, linking a theory of natural selection to questions of both animal and human behaviour. The idea is that human genes have been selected because of the ways they have encouraged types of human behaviour. We will naturally, it is said, favour kin, for evolutionary reasons, since they share our genes. Mechanisms encouraging such favouritism will have the effect of helping to spread our own genes, including those encouraging favouring kin. Those who do not look after their offspring are not going to have any to transmit their genes to future generations. Thus the idea of 'kin selection' has been developed. We naturally, too, it is claimed, favour those who return our help. We are reluctant to assist those who are, in turn, unready to reciprocate. Those who help others without getting corresponding benefits will not do as well as those who are more grudging. They will be squandering their efforts, from an evolutionary point of view, and will not survive as well, nor have as many descendants to transmit their genes, including those encouraging caution in choosing who to help. Thus the idea of 'reciprocal altruism' is born.

How far this takes us into the sphere of morality is contentious, since much genuine altruism is still left unexplained. Nevertheless, the claim is that there has been an even development from animals to humans in the production of moral responses and insights. Thus Frans de Waal, a noted expert on apes, writes:

> Although I shy away from calling chimpanzees 'moral beings', their psychology contains many of the ingredients that, if also present in the progenitor of humans and apes, must have allowed our ancestors to develop a moral sense. Instead of seeing morality as a radically new invention, I tend to view it as a natural outgrowth of ancient social tendencies.[3]

Cooperation, sympathy, eagerness to resolve conflict and many other of the building blocks of morality are demonstrated by de Waal as present in ape behaviour. He tries to show how in morality humans are merely using tendencies to react to each other and to the world, which are already present in some animals. It is being claimed that morality is an outgrowth of a human nature that itself is derived from animal nature. This analysis in some ways converges with the expectations of what neo-Darwinian theory would expect. It makes morality an integral part of a human nature, which has evolved through natural selection to form part of the fairly stable characteristics of what it is to be human. It is a part of the objective features of the world, which can be investigated by science.

Morality (or its beginnings), it is suggested, is a development of our animal nature, and is not opposed to it. This goes against many pictures of our moral impulses, which typically see them as trying to control and restrain our animal lusts and passions. Our natural state, it is thought, is one where life is nasty, brutish and short, where there is a war of all against all. That was certainly Hobbes's view in the seventeenth century, and, from Plato to Freud, thinkers have believed that our natural desires have to be restrained, and directed by reason. Yet views of a 'state of nature' have varied over the centuries, with some thinking it inherently dangerous, and in need of rational control. Others have had conceptions of 'noble savages', and even thought an initial state of nature might be desirable.

De Waal is, at least partly, in the latter camp. He sees some basic impulses, which we share with higher apes, as partly constitutive of our moral nature. Apes may not be conscious moral agents, but they can show sympathy and concern for each other in ways that humans echo. Our animal nature is not intrinsically evil, according to this view. Yet for others, the stress on furthering selfish interests, which evolutionary theory makes, suggests a lack of genuine concern for other people, except as an instrument for pursuing one's own good, or that of relatives. The very idea of the 'selfish gene' has encouraged a view of evolution as ensuring that those who act on such a policy, consciously or unconsciously, are the ones who survive and have most descendants. 'Selfishness' seems endemic in human nature, and it is easy to see this scientific picture as an analogue of the theological doctrine of original sin. It seems as if selfishness, and the uncompromising pursuit of one's own advantage, is 'natural'.

Once again, though, the vagueness of the word 'natural' is clear. For de Waal, mutual cooperation and sympathy, and the need, even in apes, for norms of social behaviour, are as ingrained as any ruthless urge to compete. For many evolutionary psychologists, morality is either reducible to the furthering of enlightened self-interest or a cloak for a selfishness that we are often (perhaps, it is said, itself for evolutionary reasons) reluctant to admit even to ourselves. According to de Waal: 'A morality exclusively concerned with individual rights tends to ignore the ties, needs and interdependencies that have marked our existence from the very beginning.'[4]

The issue is not just what we find natural, or what comes easily to us. Part of the problem with the natural status of feelings and judgements is whether we are held in thrall by them, or can control and guide them. How far can we do anything about 'natural' urges to be selfish? We may show capacities, like the great apes, for empathy, sympathy and mutual aid. Are those interesting facts about us, or can those characteristics be fostered and encouraged? It seems inappropriate to judge chimpanzees as capable of moral judgement. Their character may be better than is acknowledged by those who talk of the 'beast' in human nature. It seems, though, to be fixed. We do not hold them morally responsible for their actions. They are not going to have serious discussions among themselves about how natural their morality is, or about their ability to control their feelings. We, on the other hand, may have the freedom and rationality to stand in judgement on our natural impulses. Morality often demands cool reflection, and an ability to stand back from ourselves, and our circumstances, and to look at the whole situation. I may be so angry that I want to punch someone on the nose, but my first impulse may lead me to something I will regret. So-called road rage, when motorists vent their frustrations on each other, may be intelligible. Given the stress generated by modern road conditions, it might even loosely be called 'natural', in the sense that it is quite common. Yet it is certainly not in our own best interests, let alone those of the other motorist.

How natural is morality, or the impulses that form its foundation? Is it to be imposed on raw human nature to control and restrain it, or does it 'naturally' grow out of it? Indeed, are humans in any sense naturally good, or, at least, more good than bad? Are we, on the other hand, in some sense basically corrupt? These two pictures have been current even within Christianity. Aquinas saw us as basically inclined to goodness, while Calvin and his followers have been more inclined to stress the selfishness (or sin) at the heart of our nature. Yet this perhaps presupposes that we know what morality is, and can identify it apart from our impulses. We seem to know which of them is in accord with morality and which not. Yet how do we know in the first place that the single-minded pursuit of self-interest is less acceptable than sympathy for others? What grounds a moral viewpoint to begin with?

Morality may be needed just to reinforce what we are naturally inclined to do anyway, if we naturally do care for others. If, though, the pessimistic view about human nature as fundamentally selfish is correct, then we are faced with the problem of the source and rational grounding of morality. It would seem to be profoundly unnatural if its function is mainly to restrain what we are naturally programmed to do. Yet it seems so central to human life, even if there is disagreement sometimes about its content, that it seems perverse to call it unnatural. Even Hume's cynical observation about the naturalness of vice only serves to emphasize our tendency to see things in terms of good and bad, right and wrong, virtue and vice. We do tend to see vice as wrong, however prevalent. We are comparing it some other, 'higher', standard. A human society in which there were no moral distinctions would not only be strange, but probably could not continue to exist. Indeed, the main problem about the relationship of morality with nature is not the question of origins. Arguments about how far humans share in an ape inheritance, which grounds their morality, or how far they have to control their animal nature leave the heart of the issue untouched. What is morality about? Does it have a particular content and how can this be established?

Morality and Natural Law

We are back with the problem created by the logical split between world and morality, between fact and value. Our values may have been constrained by our evolutionary history, but unless we accept an absolute determinism, that cannot be the end of the story. Why should we value one thing over another, or recommend one course of action rather than another? The issue is whether the world itself can constrain or guide the content of moral belief, or whether it is pure convention. Do we merely agree that murder and rape are not to be tolerated, in the same way that we agree to keep to one side of the road or another?

The term 'natural law' has already been use to describe the regularities of the physical world. 'Law' in that context was descriptive, not prescriptive, even if the physical world is not an utterly predictable machine. Yet in morality the term has been used prescriptively, telling us what we ought to be doing, rather than just what usually happens. St Thomas Aquinas writes that 'in speaking of human nature, we may refer either to what is proper to humanity, or to that which humans have in common with other animals'.[5] Aquinas concludes that from the first point of view 'all sins in so far as they are against reason are also against nature'. We have, he believes, a natural tendency to act according to reason; 'that is to say, according to nature'. The implication is that what is natural is to act as we ought to, and not as people often do. The 'natural' thing is to act in accordance with our nature, and not to go against it, as we are able to do.

Many are chary of this kind of talk of what is natural and unnatural. Aquinas in the passage just quoted goes on to talk of what we have in common with animals, and in that context, he refers to special sins against nature, giving homosexual practices as an instance. The stress again would be not on what does happen, whether in animals or humans, but on what ought to happen. The concept of the natural is being used to recommend and advise, not simply to describe what happens. The controversial use of the term is obvious. Indeed, people's willingness over the centuries to accept the 'natural' inferiority of women, or the 'natural' state of slavery, can also warn us against too facile an appeal to nature to justify particular practices and beliefs and condemn others.

Whatever the pitfalls in using an appeal to nature as a stick with which to beat ethical opponents, a total refusal to do so suggests that morality can have nothing to do with the way the world is. It suggests that 'nature', or 'what happens', must be irrelevant for morality. If, on the contrary, the world's events do affect us, they must do so in ways that are good and ways that are bad. We cannot be indifferent. We are born with definite tendencies, likes and dislikes. We become hungry and thirsty. We need shelter and companionship. We want to look after our children. The world can help us and hinder us in all this. We can see that some desires are more helpful than others in guiding us to what is in our interests. We tend to like sweet things, no doubt for evolutionary reasons, but giving in too much to such a desire can be bad for our health. Reason shows us that what we like cannot be the whole story. Not everything we may choose may be equally good for us.

We may be constrained by the nature of the physical world, or the 'laws of nature', but when it comes to satisfying our desires, or making rational decisions about what is good, there are no such constraints. We are free to take paths that may be harmful just as we can choose the beneficial ones. In this sense, 'natural law' does not constrain, let alone determine, action. Yet it does embody basic facts about the world, which we cannot gainsay. Our choices are ours, but they cannot change the way the world works. In this sense, 'natural law' is a shorthand phrase not for what has to happen, but for the way in which occurrences in the world are not as detached from human interests as a dichotomy between fact and values might have us believe. This means that they may not be morally neutral. Nature can have a major effect on human welfare. Since morality itself has to be concerned with what is good and bad, beneficial and harmful, to humans, it cannot disregard nature. These matters are not the consequence of arbitrary choice, but are built into the very fabric of the world. Just as actions can bring benefits, they can incur costs, and both are the result of the way the world works. This is not necessarily to sign up to a particular metaphysical vision. The benefits and costs may often be very apparent to anyone. There may be debate about how they are each to be weighted, and whether the costs are worth incurring, but often it is clear enough that there are costs. Similarly, benefits can usually be recognized as such.

Sometimes we may favour something, and be willing to incur the costs of attaining it. Reference to 'natural law' does not take away the burden of ethical decisions. It does, though, give up the pretence that the world is irrelevant, or ethically neutral. We cannot make 'existential' choices in a vacuum. Our choices, and our actions, have effects, which can rebound on us for good and ill. Talk of costs and benefits suggests that we can go against natural law, in the sense that we are, to use another idiom, going against the grain of nature. We can do this, and it might at times be right to do so. For good evolutionary reasons, we may naturally find the sight of blood repugnant. Yet anyone who wants to be a nurse, let alone a surgeon, would be well advised to surmount any initial adverse reaction. There is a 'natural' cost to be paid, but few would suggest that, from a moral point of view, surgery is to be ruled out because it is unnatural, or evokes feelings of disgust. There is an obvious sense in saying that cutting someone open is, to the highest degree, unnatural, but it may save a life.

There is a long tradition in philosophy, emanating from Aristotle, that takes 'nature' to be not so much what happens, but what is supposed to happen, when things are working as they are meant to be. In this sense, surgery can be seen as supporting nature, rather than going against it, in that it helps a body to function properly. All this invokes conceptions of purpose and teleology, which modern science has been anxious to excise. Science's preoccupation with alleged 'neutral' facts is the source of much trouble. Even the notion of health invokes a standard of what ought to happen. A diseased heart, which is not pumping blood round the body efficiently, is not behaving as it should. Medicine exists to restore bodily organs, and indeed people, to health. Without some standard as to how a body is supposed to work, medicine itself becomes problematic. There can be no way of gauging how to put something right, if there is no conception of what the proper function of a body, and its parts, might be.

This ought to be obvious. Those who suffer illness or disease, or some disability, are not able to live life as they wish or as they ought to be able to. They cannot live according to their nature. Someone with one leg cannot run. Someone who is blind cannot see. Someone who is deaf cannot hear. Yet many are so anxious to avoid any adverse judgment on those who suffer some disability or handicap that there is often a reluctance to admit that some people are, in the relevant sense, lacking capabilities and skills that 'nature' intended them to have. This claim is replete with assumptions about purpose, but one does not need any religious background to see that humans have evolved naturally so as to have certain abilities, and that those who lack them lack something important.

From a moral point of view such people are in no way worth less than 'normal' people. They may need, and be entitled to, greater attention from the rest of us. What, however, is at stake is whether we can recognize that, for example, someone deaf lacks something important. It would be desirable if they could hear, and if medical intervention, or technology, can help them, so much the better. This may seem obvious but it can be contested. Deaf parents may want a deaf child, who could take a full part in the 'deaf community' and would not be estranged from themselves. Yet most would be horrified that deafness should not be seen as something bad, to be avoided if possible. It seems, in the deepest sense, 'unnatural'.

Another contentious example is that of Siamese or conjoined twins. Should they be separated, even if at major risk of life to either or both? Certainly it would seem that together it is impossible for them to live a normal life. There seems nothing more unnatural than for two people to be permanently joined together. A natural life is surely one lived by individuals, who may relate to each other, but who are distinct from each other and able to act independently. Yet some argue against assuming that such twins must always be separated, not just because of the dangers of the process and the risk of death, but because it is imposing a particular picture of the normal life, which is to be lived by atomic individuals, on others. Who are we to decide, it will be asked, what is good for others, perhaps even at the expense of their life?

Without the ability to invoke some standard for what counts as normal, and natural, we have no means apart from an individual's own decision, or from an arbitrary social convention, of coming to any view about what ought to be done. This may seem democratic, and to show a proper respect for the rights of an individual (assuming we know what they are). It is in fact another consequence of emptying the world of value, and making each individual the sole repository and source of moral choices. Then the choices have to be made in a fundamentally arbitrary manner. I may feel strongly about something, but if that cannot be judged against any external criterion, morality is built on the shifting sands of individual judgement and its passing whims, or of the passing fashions and fancies of a particular society. That is all we can be left with if no appeal can be made to any standard of normality or of nature. Since individuals differ in their views, and it is difficult to define what a society or community is, we are bound to be tossed away from the calm waters of rational discussion into the maelstrom of political negotiation. Reason becomes supplanted by political power.

Notes

1   David Hume, *A Treatise of Human Nature, III, I*, in A. MacIntyre (ed.), *Hume's Ethical Writings*, Macmillan, New York, 1965, p. 200.
2   For further discussion of neo-Darwinism and morality see my *The Shaping of Man: Philosophical Aspects of Sociobiology*, Chapter 8, Blackwell, Oxford, 1982; my *Ideas of Human Nature*, 2nd edn, Chapter 8 on Darwin, Blackwell, Oxford, 1999; and my *Understanding Social Science*, 2nd edn, Blackwell, Oxford, 2001, Chapters 8 and 9.
3   Frans de Waal, *The Ape and the Sushi Master*, Penguin, Harmondsworth, 2001, p. 350.
4   Frans de Waal, *Good Natured*, Harvard University Press, Cambridge, MA, 1996, p. 167.
5   St Thomas Aquinas, *Summa Theologica*, 1a, 2ae, 943.

2

Human nature and natural law

What Is Natural Law?

Stress on the importance of decisions about 'values' has, in the present day, put a focus on the judgement of individuals in the field of morality. It has prevented us from asking whether such judgements are true or false, or what in the world might be relevant to questions of truth. The idea that we should be constrained by anything outside ourselves has seemed an unwarranted limitation on our freedom. In particular, any idea that 'nature' itself carries with it any moral weight has been scorned. Natural law can describe and predict. It should in no sense prescribe. However, these are modern notions. The idea of natural law in moral matters has been connected historically with that of natural law in the world at large. Very often, a perceived order and regularity in the workings of the physical world has been linked with notions of purpose and of moral order. Yet during science's long march since the seventeenth century, there has been a ruthless removal of such ideas of purpose (or teleology) from the landscape. Moral notions are not measurable or quantifiable. They are not susceptible to scientific verification. Natural law has come to be seen as the description of mechanisms, or regularities, without any idea that one is better or worse than another. Neo-Darwinian attempts to explain the mechanisms at work, which govern a genetic influence on our moral decision-making, are the inevitable outcome of this approach. Even morality itself, it seems, is to be explained in terms of 'blind', non-purposive, natural events under genetic control.

When humans are brought into the picture, it becomes very much more difficult to see neutral descriptions of processes as adequate to describing human life. Some things are better for us, and others are worse. We have to decide for ourselves which are which and endure the consequences. We have to live a human way of life which is constrained by the needs and interests of our common nature. Yet at the same time we are free to make the wrong decisions. If we are not totally programmed by our biology, we have to understand that, even so, our freedom is not absolute. There are biological, social and other costs to be paid if we pursue our freedom without any regard to the context in which we act.

Some protest at the concept of a human nature shared by us all. Who we think we are, we may be told, depends on our society. Yet without a common humanity there would be no basic standard to which we could appeal to enable us to understand each other, whether within the confines of our own society or across cultures and societies. History would be a puzzle, because we could never generalize across generations. Other cultures would be separated by unbridgeable chasms created by different reactions and thought processes. Translations between different human languages would become impossible. Philosophical positions that stress the way that 'human' beings are created by their social, cultural or historical context start producing all these difficulties. The very idea of the human becomes lost.

Modern exponents of natural law in a moral context point to the central importance of human nature. One writer claims: 'A natural law theory asserts that the fundamental reasons for action are certain goods that are grounded in the nature of human beings.'[1] Without such a nature there could be no idea of any goods. Yet the antiseptic, non-moral conception of the world favoured by science makes this kind of view seem untenable. Moral 'facts' can seem to have nothing in common with human nature. The latter appears to be an objective part of the world, while the former are despatched to the realm of subjective 'values', or whims. The division between so-called 'naturalism' and 'non-naturalism', description and prescription, scientific assessment and moral advice, has seemed absolute.

All that, however, depends on a philosophical dogma, which refuses to entertain the possibility that any part of nature, even human nature, has any moral relevance, let alone as a part of any moral order. Unless, though, morality is a system of totally arbitrary human reactions, perhaps based on emotion, it has to have some connection with what is actually good or bad for humans. What harms us or benefits us cannot be irrelevant, and that in turn depends on some conception of humanity and its role. Even agreed biological needs must be too important for morality to ignore. That is why moral theories have often been occupied with ideas of human 'flourishing'.

If we do not know what it is for a human to flourish, even in the simplest sense, we cannot know what is good or bad for us. We cannot know what morality should promote or what it should prevent.

The relevance of substantive notions about human nature to morality must be clear. Different views about what constitutes human nature inevitably affect our idea of flourishing. A materialist, believing in this life alone, will have a different view from a Christian, who sees this life as part of a wider whole. A follower of Aristotle will have a different idea from an admirer of Darwin. Yet, even so, there are always going to be limits on what could legitimately count as flourishing. Someone dying a painful death at a young age could not be said in this sense to be flourishing. Even if that were demanded in pursuit of some greater good, it is still something that must be seen as bad. That is what makes it self-sacrifice. There have to be limits in the way in which what is good or bad in human nature can be interpreted or conceived. In the end we reach bedrock, whatever our religious or philosophical views. Certain things just are against our interests as humans, whatever we may think. That is why desire alone is not a guide for human morality. It has to be tempered, at the very least, by a rational assessment of the longer-term implications of getting what we want.

A doctrine of natural law normally takes its stand on an assertion of the centrality and importance of human nature for ethics. The latter provides it with its subject matter. Its vision is a moral one, and not a narrowly scientific one. It does not just provide a 'neutral' description of what happens to us but involves recommendations that we should live in accord with our nature, and not go against its grain. There are, however, often other elements in a natural law theory. Natural law can in fact be seen on three distinct levels. Apart from questions of human nature, theorists can point out how humans naturally accept basic (or first) principles of, say, justice. That the innocent ought not to be punished is just one of many principles that may gather wide assent just because they seem right. In addition, as Russell Hittinger, a contemporary American writer, puts it, 'natural law can be approached not only as order in the mind or order in nature but also as the ordinance of a divine lawgiver'.[2] His conclusion is that discourse about natural law 'can gravitate toward any one or a combination of these three foci: law in the human mind, in nature, and in the mind of God'.[3]

Many might look to 'nature' for guidance as to how we should behave, while remaining sceptical about the ability of the human mind to abide by fixed 'first principles'. It might seem plausible to say that humans generally have a strong sense of what is often called 'natural justice'. They can instinctively react against great wrongs. Yet it might be that what is obviously unjust and self-evidently wrong in one society is acceptable in another. Building morality on the foundations of our intuitions and upon appeals to self-evidence is always a risky business. If certain things are that self-evident, why, anyway, does injustice occur? These are large issues, but any doctrine of natural law has to take human rationality seriously, even if it is unwilling to take at face value what passes for common sense in a given society at a particular time. Human reason, it will hold, has within its power the ability to discover what is good and bad.

Reason and Natural Law

The fact that theories of natural law can gravitate in different directions can give rise to confusion among its supporters and opponents. Some would see it as a covertly religious position, and indeed, if the role of God as law-giver is stressed, it can become that. Yet others would put natural law in a much more secular context. This can mean that the rhetoric of natural law (and natural, or human, rights) is used on the public stage without any theistic overtones at all. This is not very surprising, as appeals to a natural law, open to everyone's reason, have traded on its independence from a doctrinal basis. Agreement has been sought about it from those of differing religious and metaphysical beliefs. This makes the theory appear as if it can stand on its own. Indeed, the next stage is to use it as a guarantee of human freedom and autonomy. In the words of Hittinger, for many, 'natural law constitutes an authority-free zone'.[4] Enlightenment philosophers were fond of imagining humans in a state of nature, sometimes thought desirable and sometimes not. The point, though, was that it was a state preceding any authority or human law. 'Nature', then, could stand for a human autonomy which religion appeared to undermine. 'Natural' reason was, it seemed, very often antagonistic to the idea of God or divine revelation, just as it was suspicious of the idea of ecclesiastical authority. The contemporary idea of rights is deeply embedded in such views, and in some people's eyes religion is itself intent on challenging human rights. This can seem highly paradoxical to those who consider that human rights depend on some wider religious view of God's concern for humans. Hittinger therefore issues this stern warning: 'When the Christian theologian plays with the modern rhetoric of natural law, he is apt to underestimate the anti-theological meanings of modern natural law (essentially man as a free agent without God).'[5]

Many contemporary theologians would echo this, and following Karl Barth, would be distrustful of the attempts of human reason to set standards on its own without the guide of revelation. The idea that goodness could be identified without explicit reference to divine revelation would be anathema. For them, philosophy itself would be suspect and would suggest efforts by humans to decide truth without reference to God. Yet, on the other side, there are many who would be equally distrustful of natural law, because they would see in it a theistic agenda. They would complain that it makes the world appear full of purpose and moral weighting in a way that only makes sense if they have been placed there by a Creator.

These disagreements occur because of basic disagreements about the character of the world. If we are creatures of a God, that must make a difference to how humans are perceived, and may influence our view of their intrinsic importance. Yet we have already seen that many questions about what is good and harmful for humans can be dealt with without addressing that question. Smoking, for instance, is a source of ill-health, whether or not God is brought into the issue. Anyone deliberately promoting smoking for personal profit could be fairly accused of doing something immoral, since, inevitably, the result will be considerable disease and suffering. Harm can be recognized very often independently of ideology and metaphysics. Our reason can be used whether or not we see it as autonomous or as a divine gift. The eighteenth-century Enlightenment grew to see it as the former, but it is important that its origins lay with a very different view. The philosophical and theological background that led to the flowering of modern science and the founding of the Royal Society, under Charles II in England, viewed reason not as an opponent of religion but as the 'candle of the Lord'. That was the slogan of the Cambridge Platonists in the middle of the seventeenth century. Reason might be fallible and only give us some knowledge, just as a candle gives off a pale and flickering light. Nevertheless, it was to be respected, precisely because it reflects the reason of the Creator. It gives us a path to truth.[6]

Natural law, it has often been held, can be recognized through reason, and, what is more, a reason to which all have access. That is no doubt why such law has appeared to be an appropriate underpinning for democracy, particularly in the United States. Questions of natural law, like the questions of human nature to which they are related, are objective in character, and open to discovery by anyone. Ideologies may produce different conceptions of human nature, but in the end they themselves have to be subject to the way the world is. They will be shown up if they operate with a wrong view of human nature. This is what has happened with Marxism. It has been implemented in disastrous ways, often culminating in oppression, mass murder and great suffering. Marxist countries have often failed in a most significant way to promote human flourishing. At a theoretical level, it failed to take seriously enough the innate selfishness of people, convincingly demonstrated in modern neo-Darwinism. The communist assumption that, if only the shackles of capitalism were removed, we would all be shown to be naturally cooperative and unselfish was not borne out in the socialist societies of Eastern Europe. So, far from class distinction being removed, a new breed of party bosses and privileged party members made the most of their opportunities at the expense of ordinary people. Peter Singer is not alone in seeing all this stemming from human nature, and in particular from a human tendency to form hierarchies. He suggests that seeing this 'as inherent in human beings helps us to understand the rapid departure from equality in the Soviet Union'.[7] In Singer's words, and they apply everywhere, 'to be blind to facts about human nature is to risk disaster'.[8]

In this case, the natural tendencies, which asserted themselves even against the pressures of society, were far from admirable. This shows that natural law should not be confused with how people naturally are inclined to behave. 'Human nature' retains a perpetual ambiguity. What is conducive to our nature is not necessarily the same as what we find it naturally easy to do. We can be our own worst enemies, reaching eagerly to what we want in ways that cause great harm to everyone. Natural law can be ignored or followed but it is not an optional extra, or a useful instrument. The laws of gravity are similarly not optional, although we can choose to ignore them. We can choose whether to step out of the upper floor of a skyscraper, but we cannot choose whether we then fall or not. We can go against the interests of our own nature, but cannot prevent the harm that will inevitably follow. Modern moral philosophy places stress on desire and choice, and often concentrates less on needs and interests. Yet even though we act because we want to, we cannot normally control the results. Our desires certainly stem from our human nature, but so do our needs. Morality has to try to draw the two closer together than they often are, by means of our reason.

Any stress on rationality engenders deep suspicion nowadays. Just because the Enlightenment restricted reason to what could be discovered by science, it was inevitable eventually that there would be a reaction. Unfortunately this all too often takes the form of an outright distrust of all reason. So-called 'postmodernism' may oppose the arrogance of those who think that a narrow concentration on scientific 'facts' exhausts our knowledge. By challenging this, however, it challenges the idea of reason, as a human capacity. Instead we are left with a multiplicity of traditions and perspectives, none of which can have any common ground on which to meet each other. The result must be catastrophic for ethics, since this places the views of any society beyond criticism from outside. It is indeed paradoxical that the rhetoric of human rights gathers pace alongside a postmodernism that decries the idea of any universal truth, or common human nature. There can, then, be no 'rights' transcending societies, and no humans to have them. Ethical discussion across the globe is only going to be possible if we recognize that we all do have something common. Natural law theorists, at least, will be able to point to our common humanity, and our shared ability to reason.

Going against the 'Grain of Nature'

Reason can help us to understand the kind of world we live in, and the costs and benefits of various kinds of action. We cannot pretend, for instance, that going against the grain of nature will not carry its costs. There are norms for living a properly functioning human life. Sometimes we deliberately flout those norms and must bear the consequences. Sometimes we have to live in ways that are less than desirable through no fault of our own. The deaf must remain deaf, even though they may obtain help from artificial aids. Deficient hearing is a fault, in the sense that we are prevented from living as we should and as we wish without adequate hearing. We cannot function properly, not least because we are cut off from ordinary communication with others. We can fall into danger, as when we do not hear vehicles coming. Whatever we might wish to say about the rights of deaf people, and the evils of discrimination, and however angry we might be about callous disregard of others' difficulties, the fact remains that they are difficulties. Deafness is an obstacle to living a life. It is in our nature to have proper hearing. The same can be said about other physical problems. A desire to treat those suffering from them with proper dignity is a different issue from deciding what is good and bad for human life. We need to see, and that is why we should give special consideration to those who cannot. Yet the desire not to give offence can easily become an unwillingness to acknowledge that there are standards of health and bodily functioning, which we need as humans in order to flourish. Without them, we face obstacles, which can be overcome and which we should be helped to overcome. Nevertheless, they are real.

Nature, in this sense, implies a standard to which humans ought to conform, even if they do not always do so. It is natural to hear, even though some are deaf. It is natural to be an individual, separate physically from others, even though there are sometimes conjoined twins. What is natural is what ought to happen if things work properly. What is it for human nature to be functioning properly? Aquinas, following Aristotle, recognized that creatures have innate tendencies to particular ends. When they are thwarted from obtaining these, for whatever reason, they are not functioning properly and will fail to flourish. The teleology inherent in this was despised by followers of Darwin, but even those who stand fully behind the theory of evolution have to recognize that humans have evolved to be a particular kind of organism, with particular needs. Neo-Darwinians press the case for the importance of human nature, against the discredited view, encouraged by empiricism, that we are born like blank slates, or pieces of white paper, on which experience alone can write. On the contrary, it is now generally recognized, partly because of research on the human genome, that all humans are born with dispositions and tendencies that can lead in particular directions. We are, to use another image, 'hard-wired' to have certain desires and needs. There are costs, both major and minor, to pay if these are not met.

Ethics cannot be neutral about this. Other things being equal, it would seem right that basic human needs and interests are met. Our desires are indeed often an indication of what is good for us. We want, and need, food and drink. It is a traditional view of moral philosophy, from Plato onwards, that desires have to be controlled by reason. That is what Aquinas thought. Since reason is what distinguishes humans from animals, it is, he thought, following Aristotle, the life which governs its activity by reason that is most natural for humans. We are then enabled to exercise our faculties properly.

The idea is that animals and other organisms have their proper nature, and cannot flourish if they are thwarted from fulfilling it. They may, for instance, be cooped up in cramped conditions through the methods of factory farming. They will not normally do as well, and, say, put on weight, as they would under more normal conditions. In the same way, humans do better if they follow their true nature. Yet this is not a blind process, since the most important element in our nature is our reason. Rationality does not and cannot, though, operate in a vacuum. It has to use our given nature as raw material. Human needs and desires – not just mine, but those of others – provide the content of morality. How do we deal with them? That is the prime task of moral thinking.

What Is Morality About?

One of the main issues in morality is why we should be concerned with other people. Why should I not just try, in an enlightened manner, to further my own desires? Even if I look at the long-term implications, I am still trying to see the world solely as it affects me, and that is egoism. It may be significant that no one usually questions why we each should be bothered about our own desires. That is just what it is to want something. It seems obvious that if I want something, I have a reason for trying to get it. Have others a reason to help me in those circumstances, or I them if they desire something? This is where our human rationality comes into play. Making exceptions in one's own favour on the simple ground that I am me is not particularly rational. Why should I alone eat when others are hungry, unless there is something special about me? Of course we each naturally want to eat, but why should I not share some of my food with others if I can? It is a function of reason to decide when and where there are special circumstances needing special treatment. Morality cannot depend on my having a sudden willingness to share. It has to be built on firmer foundations than that. The idea that I matter, and others do not, may be seductive. The question is: what could give it any rational justification?

We are, though, still free to ignore the subject matter of morality, even if to some extent it is presented to us by the facts about human nature. This is the insight of those who stress the absolute freedom we possess as human beings to form our own moral judgements, and our own moral vision. People do differ in their moral judgements, but we may find the judgements fallible. They concern what lies beyond themselves. They concern nature, both our human nature and the way the world impinges on it. There is something against which they can be judged.

Seen in this light, morality is neither a subjective whim nor a passing fashion. It has to involve judgements about what is good and bad for humans. We cannot make the world, or our own natures, always conform to our will. There will be costs to pay, as well as benefits to be acquired. These are not constituted by our understanding. The same point applies to questions about our interest. The fact that I do not concern myself with some future harm that could befall me does not mean that I will not suffer it. If I prefer the present pleasure of smoking to a possible future threat to health, a decision to smoke will not in any way prevent what may be a premature death. The decision may indeed help to bring it about. If young people seek out pop music that is literally deafening, and then become deaf in later years, they are responsible for producing objective harm on themselves. Nature surrounds us, constrains us and can kill us. Our moral freedom cannot gainsay it.

The old idea of natural law held within it the idea that we cannot set ourselves apart from the world in which we live. We are an integral part of it, and our moral freedom cannot allow us to pretend otherwise. In fact, natural law, with the costs and benefits of behaving in particular ways, is open for everyone to see. It requires no special theological or metaphysical doctrine. As Aquinas remarked, 'in questions of theory, truth is the same for everyone'.[9] He contrasted this with questions about action, where he recognized that the application of common, basic, principles would not always give rise to the same decision. Costs and benefits may be constant, but decisions about how to deal with them may depend on particular circumstances. The latter change cases. He saw the difficulty of applying fixed rules to particular cases, even though natural law became later codified by the Roman Catholic Church. It is a mistake to think that the natural law has to be understood in absolute terms, governing our every action, just as it is a mistake to see it as dictating our actions in a determinist sense.

References to natural law in a moral context guide our decisions by reminding us that we are, at least, natural beings set in a natural environment. Our nature is given to us, just as to some extent our environment is. We can change some of the latter, and voices are beginning to be heard suggesting that we can use our new-found knowledge of the genetic constitution of humans even to change our human nature. The risks and dangers inherent in this should be obvious. As things stand, however, many of the costs and benefits resulting from our present actions are not under our control.

If, though, natural law does not govern our choices in any strong sense, how does it differ from a utilitarianism that demands that we weigh the consequences of our actions? Given that natural law encourages, even enjoins, the use of reason, is it any different from ordinary utilitarian reckoning? Many would see natural law and utilitarianism as opposite to each other. Yet if natural law merely sets in place principles, which can be applied in different ways in different situations, and if it accepts that sometimes it is justifiable to pay even high costs, what is the difference? There is certainly a stress on principle, but rule utilitarianism would claim that it too sets great store by the beneficial consequences of applying rules.

One answer is that it is rare to find absolute differences between moral theories. Utilitarianism does not simply say that consequences matter, while everyone else denies that. The issue is not their importance but whether they are the only thing that matters. Many would feel that there is something intrinsically wrong with doing something unnatural, and that there is an intrinsic danger in going against the grain of nature. It is not just that bad consequences tend to happen sometimes. The very act, whatever it may be, disrupts natural processes in ways that may well be harmful, but may be unforeseeable. As such it involves a level of risk that cannot be assessed by utilitarian criteria, but should itself be a warning.

A constant worry about the utilitarian stress on the moral relevance of consequences is that it assumes that we are likely to know what the consequences are. A stress on natural law may advise a certain caution. If we go against nature, or interfere with it, we are initially setting in train a series of events which, by definition, do not normally happen. This itself produces a novel situation, in which there may be hidden dangers. Going with the grain of nature means that we use natural processes in ways which are not unusual but have been tested through evolutionary processes. The possibility of great harm has been winnowed out. In the light of modern technology, new opportunities seem to provide the possibility of, say, medical advances. Yet we must also realize that interference in natural processes, perhaps by importing genes across species boundaries, may create a new combination of circumstances that we cannot foresee but that may be extremely harmful. Modern methods of farming, with the use of 'unnatural' feed for cattle, helped to precipitate the BSE (or 'mad cow') crisis in the United Kingdom in the 1990s. It may have seemed a good idea to feed herbivore cattle with animal products, such as chopped up brains, but this resulted in a disease that not only harmed the cattle, but apparently jumped the species barrier to humans.

No doubt utilitarian considerations at the time only concentrated on the financial benefits of new methods of feeding. They did not dwell on the then unknown dangers. A rational utilitarian, dealing with knowable consequences, would no doubt have advocated the 'unnatural' feed. It probably appeared financially cost-effective. Anyone more willing to think in terms of natural processes might have wondered about the ultimate costs of disrupting them. Much of the feeling against what is unnatural may stem from a fear that utilitarianism and allied moral positions are far too optimistic about the scope of human knowledge. We should all want to do good and minimize harm. The issue is what that means, and how we should achieve it. The stress on the natural is one way of restraining human optimism, and even human arrogance. It reminds us that we are set in a world that does not always conform to our wishes. Even if our only aim is to further human interests, we have to recognize how they are embedded in a wider whole, which does not always react as we might expect.

Notes

1   Mark C. Murphy, *Natural Law and Practical Rationality*, Cambridge University Press, Cambridge, 2002, p. 2.
2   R. Hittinger, *The First Grace: Rediscovering the Natural Law in a Post-Christian World*, ISI Books, Wilmington, DE, 2003, p. 4.
3   Ibid.
4   Ibid., p. xii.
5   Ibid., p. 37.
6   See C. Taliaferro and A. Teply (eds), *Cambridge Platonist Spirituality*, Paulist Press, New York, 2004.
7   Peter Singer, *A Darwinian Left*, Weidenfeld and Nicholson, London, 1999, p. 59.
8   Ibid., p. 38.
9   St Thomas Aquinas, *Summa Theologica*, 1a, 2ae, 943.

3

Human rights

The Political Context

Views about natural law have become closely connected with talk of 'natural rights', which was given great impetus by the English philosopher of the seventeenth century, John Locke. He in turn is often credited with having provided the philosophical basis for the American Declaration of Independence. Such talk gets its cogency from the implication that 'rights' are deeply ingrained in the nature of things. Above all, of course, they are then linked to our own nature as human beings. Yet this is not just of historical interest, since appeals to rights form a large part of contemporary moral language. 'Human rights' are the currency of much contemporary moral discourse, and form a potent weapon in international relations. People get particularly indignant when they feel their rights have not been met. Moral campaigns are often couched in the language of human rights. At a time when natural law itself is often neglected, this may seem curious. Yet in politics the language of rights, both within nations and in relations between them, has its effect. It can empower victims, and give them an opportunity to appeal to standards beyond their own social context.

What precisely is being appealed to? What are human rights, and how can they be enforced? What are they grounded in (if anything) and how can we tell the difference between a legitimate and a spurious right? 'Rights' are often appealed to in a vague way. Increasingly the laws of various countries are required to take notice of human rights, and there is a major question of interpretation. Often the rights are underspecified. The United States has always allowed judges to veto legislation on the ground that it transgresses basic constitutional rights. In the United Kingdom the doctrine was always that Parliament was sovereign, but in recent years judicial review of legislation has become increasingly common. This follows the Human Rights Act of 1998, which brings the European Convention on Human Rights into the domestic law of the United Kingdom. Even the decisions of Parliament can be scrutinized in the courts to ensure that they meet certain standards derived from human rights. Canada had previously taken a similar path, by subjecting its laws to requirements about human rights, under the Canada Act and the Canadian Charter of Rights and Freedoms of 1982.

However, while legislation can grant certain civil rights in a particular country, the idea of human rights is much harder to make explicit. Simply because they often appear as standards legislation has to meet, rather than being codified in legislation, rights are by their very nature hard to pin down in practical terms. Even if one has a list, and a government prepared to implement it, this is still a long way from having clear and enforceable legislation. As Russell Hittinger points out, 'One needn't be a sceptic about natural or human rights to understand the problem posed by under-specified rights, which so often find expression in bills and charters of rights.'[1] His point is that one still needs a specific legal procedure to put into practice the ideals promulgated. Without it, one is in a world of unfocused moral outrage, because, as Hittinger says, 'people believe they have a right prior to anyone knowing precisely what it is'. Yet we then have a situation in which moral claims can be made, and indignation expressed, without any clear responsibility for action by anyone. This is bound to undermine morality. As Hittinger says, rights have to be given a proper specification. Otherwise, as he puts it, 'no one can know who is bound to do (or not to do) *what* to *whom*'.[2]

What, then, is the point of talking of human rights? Once in Britain, during a bakers' strike, an irate trade union leader, when interviewed, proclaimed that time off for bakers on a 'bank holiday' was a basic human right. He seemed oblivious of the fact that the idea of a bank holiday is a peculiarly British one, and that there could be no question of a universal right to have that particular Monday off. Yet if human rights claim anything, they have to claim universal applicability across all nations and times. A core part of a commitment to human rights is just that there are ways no human should be treated anywhere at any time. Our common humanity is ground enough for proper treatment.

The union leader was not being as ridiculous as might first appear, however. Article 24 of the United Nations Declaration of Human Rights proclaims that 'everyone has the right to rest and leisure, including reasonable limitation of working hours and periodic holidays with pay'. While the Declaration no doubt did not have British bank holidays specifically in mind, the trade unionist might legitimately feel that this was just a local application of that general principle. This, though, raises the question of how it is decided what rights there are. Where do they come from?

No one familiar with international politics in the contemporary world will have any doubt of the importance of human rights. One has only to visit the United Nations in New York, and see the Declaration hung in a series of frames along one of the walls, to be in no doubt that the idea of human rights is at the centre of the work of the United Nations and its agencies. Yet there is a paradox. There are still many abuses of human rights, many of them perpetrated by the actions of some of the very governments whose flags fly outside the headquarters. The United Nations, in other words, proclaims something which is not practised, and may not be believed, by all of its members.

One of the reasons for this is evident in a comparison of the United Nations Declaration of Human Rights with the American Declaration of Independence. The former was adopted in 1948, when the shadows of the Holocaust and other terrible suffering in the Second World War lay over the nations. It begins by referring to the 'inherent dignity and the equal and inalienable rights of all members of the human family'. It continues by saying that it is essential that these rights be protected by the rule of law. Yet this raises the question of which law, that of an individual nation or something constituted on an international basis. It appears preferable that, as long as there are sovereign states, their law codifies basic rights, but we are then left with the issue of what happens when a 'rogue' state refuses to.

In the United States, the Declaration of Independence memorably says: 'We hold these truths to be self-evident, that all men are created equal, that they are endowed by their Creator with certain inalienable rights; that among these are life, liberty and the pursuit of happiness.' The first sentences had referred to 'the laws of nature and nature's God', and the Declaration ends with an assertion of the 'protection of Divine Providence'. The whole pronouncement was based on a belief in a God who had made humans, and who guaranteed the worth of each individual. Some of the signatories to the Declaration of Independence may have had a general belief in a Creator without necessarily appealing to Christian revelation. Many, however, were devout Christians, and intended the Declaration to be seen in a Christian context, while still embracing those of other faiths.

The United Nations Declaration, on the other hand, takes the worth of individual humans for granted, simply referring to a 'recognition' of their inherent dignity. Yet it does not say where this comes from or why we have it. We just do. Article 1 says that 'all are born free and equal in dignity and rights'. Why is this so? The next sentence significantly reads: 'They are endowed with reason and conscience, and should act towards one another in a spirit of brotherhood.' The word 'endowed' calls into question who or what has endowed us. One conclusion might be that we have been made in the image of God. Yet the Declaration does not say that, despite the religious overtones of the word 'brotherhood'. It implicitly invokes the concept of the 'fatherhood' of God. A possible grounding for our rights is thus hinted at but not stated.

There were good political reasons for this. Whatever the ultimate inspiration for the idea of rights, it had to gain acceptance even by such nations as the atheist Soviet Union. It appealed to a heritage of natural law, without inquiring into its possible grounding. This, though, makes the Declaration vulnerable at a theoretical level, since when the idea of human rights is challenged, there seems no way of defending it, beyond pointing to international agreement.

The Status of Rights

Some have applauded a 'pragmatic' approach to the idea of justifying human rights. Michael Ignatieff says: 'Pragmatic silence on ultimate questions has made it easier for a global human rights culture to emerge.'[3] Since there is little likelihood of universal agreement about any particular foundation for rights, such as a theistic one, it is better, so it appears, merely to seek what agreement we can. It is always tempting to duck difficult moral questions, and reduce them to the political issue of obtaining some kind of consensus. This is a prime example. We let go of any idea of justifying our moral principles concerning rights, and merely try to negotiate what agreement we can. We are content that a view is held and feel no need to inquire into why it should be.

Anthony Appiah also defends a similar freedom from what he terms 'high doctrine in the development of the international law of human rights'.[4] His view is that 'we should be able to defend our treaties by arguing that they offer people protections against governments that most of their citizens desire – protections important enough that they also want other peoples, through their governments, to help sustain them'. It seems that rights are to be rights because people (or, at least, some people) want them.

Talk of rights speaks, Appiah thinks, to those from a wide variety of traditions, and we can gain support for human rights 'because of that resonating agreement'.[5] The universality of human rights seems thus to depend on an empirical fact about widespread agreement. They are important because many think they are. They are supported because they are supported. At best, they are conventions, like the rules of the road, and like them, they may be different in some places.

Appiah, and others, do not consider this approach to be deficient in any way, but see it as a virtue. Pragmatists, particularly in the American tradition, are notoriously suspicious of metaphysics, and always prefer the solid ground of actual agreement and concrete practice. Why, though, should we agree in the first place, and how should we deal with those who do not accept what we say? This is not an academic question in international affairs, and, unless we just resort to force to impose our point of view, there may seem no way forward. Anyone can use force to spread any cause, and it is hard to see any difference between naked imperialism and an imposition of 'our' will about human rights. Only an appeal to some rational justification would distinguish our position from that of those who are merely doing what they want, and exercising power for its own sake.

Appiah's position is that human rights can be sustained without metaphysical debate. He affirms: 'Since metaphysical debate is unlikely to yield consensus, let us proceed to endorse and enforce them without it as much as we can.'[6] No doubt the framers of the United Nations Declaration had that in mind. The problem, however, remains that rights based on a consensus do not fare too well when a consensus is not forthcoming. Why, too, should anyone agree about human rights in the first place if there is no reason to do so? The powerful, in particular, can impose their will by force. Metaphysical foundations are not useless bits of machinery unconnected to anything. To take another image, they support the edifice. They give reasons for respecting rights. Otherwise they will only be upheld as long as they happen to be upheld. Any consensus can be transitory and unreliable. Once one has given up one's moral principles by treating moral beliefs as items for political negotiation, politics cannot be controlled by morality. Moral positions become one element in a wider political process.

The universality of human rights becomes a dubious notion in these circumstances. Rights could only be universal if there was a universal consensus. Without it, they result from political negotiation, instead of guiding it. Any idea of universal rights has to be rooted in something beyond the shifting wishes and desires of various political groupings. It has instead to be linked to the very idea of being human. The idea of universality depends on that of a universal moral order to which humans are subject, whether they realize it, or want to be, or not. Such universality has to go much deeper than the mere fact of wide agreement. The whole point of the assertion of human rights is that they apply even when they are not recognized. Those who do not agree about them ought to. There just are ways in which people ought to be treated simply in virtue of their being human. This makes it clear that the issue revolves around what it is to be human, and why our common humanity is so special. We are back with the various claims of natural law, and the religious answer given by the American Founders is just one attempt to meet that problem.

A pragmatist basis for rights, saying that we value human rights because we do, may work in a society where there is widespread recognition of them. Similarly, when everyone takes for granted the importance of our shared human characteristics, it may appear to make sense to say that we, as humans, as a matter of fact just do value each other, and rate ourselves as more important than animals. It is part our basic intuitions, or our human prejudice. This all suggests, however, that reason, or questions about the nature of the world, have little to do with it. It is all a matter of how we feel. It may perhaps be possible to build a natural law theory about the value we place on our fellow human beings, based on such inbuilt moral reactions. We live in a world, however, where the task is not to explain to ourselves the moral judgements we do make, but to persuade others who are opposed to them. We are confronted by widespread moral disagreement, and it is idle to pretend that this does not extend to the whole notion of human rights. Saying that we value them because we do will not help us to confront those in our own countries, and also throughout the world, who may ignore rights, or, more threateningly, challenge the whole idea.

What Counts as a Right?

Linked with difficulties about the status of rights is the problem of demarcation. What is to count as a basic right? The United Nations Declaration, the key document for so many, is instructive. Starting with rights to life, liberty and security, it quickly ventures into controversial territory. Article 16 asserts that 'the family is the natural and fundamental group unit of society and State'. There may be some equivocation about what a 'family' is, but the invocation of what is natural suggests a nod to natural law, and a traditional view of a biologically linked set of arrangements for the rearing of children. 'Family' can come to mean any temporary social grouping, particularly if children are included, but such arbitrary and shifting groups can hardly be regarded as 'natural'.

When the Declaration moves from negative rights to more substantial ones, things become even more controversial. Negative rights are designed to protect us from others and to preserve our role as free agents. No one should, for instance, be a slave. Positive rights to social justice are more difficult to deal with. We are told in Article 22 that everyone has a right to social security, and it is clear that this has an economic dimension. Similarly, everyone has a right to work (Article 23), even when, it seems, for economic reasons there are no jobs. Parents have 'prior' rights to choose the kind of education given to their children (Article 26). That seems to cut across the protests of those who do not wish to see the provision of education fragmented on religious, racial or other lines. It may seem to safeguard private, fee-paying education.

These rights have been codified into two Covenants, adapted in 1966 by the United Nations General Assembly. The International Covenant on Civil and Political Rights is trumpeted by the United Nations as 'a landmark in the efforts of the international community to promote human rights'.[7] In the UN's own words, 'it defends the right to life, and stipulates that no individual can be subjected to torture, enslavement, forced labour and arbitrary detention or be restricted from such freedoms as movement, expression and association'. The hope is that parties to the Covenant will enact legislation to uphold these rights, but it is remarkable how many of the signatories do not attempt to live up to these admirable aspirations.

The second International Covenant, on economic, social and cultural rights, was designed 'to ensure the protection of individuals as full persons, based on a perspective in which people can enjoy rights, freedoms and social justice simultaneously'.[8] However, rights are piled on rights. It is not now just a matter of individual freedom. The appeal to social justice makes explicit demands for an adequate standard of living, the right to take part in cultural life, the right to social insurance and the right to the highest attainable standard of physical and mental health. The right to enjoy the benefits of scientific progress is also there, and so it goes on. Aims that are morally worthy, though perhaps on occasion controversial, become rights that all have. Everyone can demand as a right the advantages that historically have only been possible for a wealthy society.

We might ask what is added to a discussion of moral aspirations if they are dubbed rights. A simple right, such as a right to life, is a precondition of everything else, and it may call attention to the fact that there are ways in which no person should be treated. Torture and slavery may fall into the same kind of category. They are both designed to restrict our freedom of action, and both turn people into things. Rights in this sense are like trumps in a card game, taking precedence over everything else. The fact that something is classed as murder or torture creates an absolute prohibition. The assumption is that human beings possess an intrinsic worth that such treatment overrides.

Once rights are multiplied, though, and everything desirable becomes an automatic right, this idea of rights as trumps has to be attenuated, if not destroyed. If all cards are trumps, there are no trumps. The more rights there are, the more likely it is that they are going to conflict, and we will have to have some principle with which to put them in order. No country's resources are unlimited, and hard choices always have to be made about, say, the respective priorities of health and education. When the United Nations refers to 'basic human rights', it lists in the same paragraph many problems concerning human deprivation, ranging from malnutrition and illiteracy to homelessness.[9] It points out that more than 1.5 billion people lack access to clean drinking water and sanitation. This all poses major challenges, of great moral concern. Yet are these needs to be considered 'rights', however important and basic they might be to human life, and thus intimately connected with ideas of human flourishing? If they are, trumps will be competing with trumps, and the result will be that the language of rights is degraded. We must distinguish between the need to outlaw slavery or torture and the laudable aspiration to provide proper drinking water. Governments may be stopped from torturing their citizens, but they may not have the economic resources to do everything that is desirable.

Who Gives Us Our Rights?

Talk of human rights grows out of an individualist vision of society, which views society not as an organic whole but as a collection of separate atoms, which are liable to collide with each other. The idea is that we are each free to choose the kind of life we wish to lead, and that 'rights' arise from the desire of citizens to receive protection from their governments. The image is that of a social contract, according to which individuals agree to live together, subject to certain provisos and prohibitions. An analogue would be the drawing up of a constitution with certain entrenched clauses, which could not be changed according to the whim of the government of the time. The source of such rights is the agreement between individuals. This picture, though, sits very uneasily with an idea of human rights, as opposed to civil rights. Citizens in a particular country might demand legal protections. The appeal to human rights, though, carries its force because its point is to transcend any particular society, and indeed all societies. Its universality suggests that it is not the product of any actual, or mythical, agreement. Rights are by their nature recognized, not constructed. Either they result from the fact of our common humanity, whether we agree about it or not, or they do not exist.

Agreements (even under United Nations auspices) do not create human rights. Otherwise those who do not consider themselves parties to the agreements can reject the whole idea without fear of criticism. Yet countries that stand aside from issues about human rights seem to be in a different moral position from, say, a country that decides not to join an agreement to have a common currency such as the euro. They appear to lay themselves open to moral criticism, and even international action. Some, however, would maintain that the talk of human rights is just a Western phenomenon, rooted in the conditions of a particular kind of society. They see quite correctly that rights are intimately related to issues concerning the fabric of a whole society.

Rights cannot exist in a social vacuum, nor can they function as just the choice of a few in any society. They require the force of a morality held in common. They can be codified in law, but even then there has to be a willingness to uphold the law. Rights do not, and cannot, create a morality, but presuppose it. They depend on a thick web of mutual relationships, where rights, duties and responsibilities are all bound up with each other. Even the United Nations Declaration dimly recognizes this, in that in Article 29 it gets round to saying that 'everyone has duties to the community in which alone the free and full development of his personality is possible'. Yet this is crucial, since the picture of individuals possessing rights on their own with an expectation that they will be given them leaves out the whole dimension of society. Morality is not just an individual matter. If it were, it

would become a matter of subjective test to be indulged in if it suits us.
Society, however, depends on a network of mutual expectations and understanding.

We all have to be seen as parts of a wider whole, on which we depend, but
to which we have to contribute. Individuals matter, but they need each
other. We are born into families, and families need the support of wider
groups. No society can exist if each member waits to be looked after by
everyone else. Morality is an active matter, connected with what we do, and
not with what is done to us. This is one of the troubling aspects of a culture
that stresses rights, and suggests that we have a claim on others to provide
them. The emphasis is put on others' duties to us and not on our responsibilities to them. The most fundamental rights are, however, preconditions
of agency. They are what is required if we ourselves can act morally. Without
life, or liberty, we can do nothing. Slavery and torture comprise attempts to
override a person's moral freedom. Arbitrary arrest, detention or exile can
also be seen as stopping us from being responsible agents. We have to be free
from interference to play any part in a society. Freedom and responsibility
are intimately intertwined.

Problems arise when rights are increased, and the freedom sought is not
just the negative one of being released from actual or metaphorical shackles,
but the positive one of giving us more of what we need to live fulfilled lives.
It may seem as if we need proper food, education, work, health care and so
on to be able to act responsibly. In a properly functioning society these all
ought to be readily available for all, and we should be working for the
improvement of the conditions of everyone. The issue is whether it is helpful
to call these 'rights'. Perhaps adequate food might be, but once a bigger
social agenda is inserted into the language of rights, things are not as clear.
People should be given the dignities and freedom that enable them to be
moral agents. That is itself a precondition for the existence of morality. It is
easy to go on from questions of what people need in order to act, and
continue to use the language of rights to refer to what it is morally desirable
for people to have. Such language, however, implies that they should expect
to receive these things. Onora O'Neill says: 'The passive culture of human
rights suggests that we can sit back, and wait for others to deliver our
entitlements. If we really want human rights, we have to act – and to
meet our duties to one another.'[10]

Rights in a society are meaningless without some recognition of who is
responsible for meeting them. The advantage of absolute prohibitions on
torture or slavery is that no one should inflict such things on anyone. The

'trumping' aspect of human rights is clear at this point. If something is torture that is enough. It is pointless going on to specify who has a duty not to inflict it. No one could under any circumstances, according to a doctrine of rights. 'Positive' rights to education and other benefits cannot have a similarly blanket application. No one should torture me, but it is not the case that everyone should educate me, or give me medical care. Such rights are aspirations for a worthwhile life, and they need to be addressed. But someone, or some body, such as a government, has to take responsibility for doing so. The real moral question cannot simply be what people are entitled to, but who has responsibility for doing something about it. For whom are we ourselves responsible? What should we be doing?

Proclaiming rights merely raises expectations and demands. It encourages many to see themselves as victims because their 'just rights' are not met. This concerns rights at their most general, even metaphysical, level. Once governments and other agencies have created legal systems which establish rights for specified people, things become easier. For instance, if someone is given a right to a pension, it has to be clear what the financial arrangements are, who is responsible for paying it and under what conditions. The system has to involve a specification of the authorities responsible for meeting the created right. 'Civil rights', the rights of a citizen in a given society, can be codified in such a way that responsibility for meeting them is clearly laid down. The courts of the particular country will be able to apply laws whose function is to specify remedies if rights are not met. Human rights, however, are by their nature so general that, if they require action by particular agencies or individuals, it is unlikely that they can be specified in any charter of rights. They thus hang in a kind of limbo, apparently setting standards without prescribing the means of meeting them.

Are 'Rights' Merely a Western Idea?

One perennial accusation made against all references to human rights is that talk of such rights merely expresses the view of a given society at a given time. This criticism has already implicitly appeared; for instance, in the idea that 'rights' stress the role of the individual too much. The suggestion is that advocacy of 'human rights' has arisen in the particular circumstances of modern Western civilization. Suspicions are aroused by how easily it fits in with a contemporary liberal agenda. Amy Gutmann writes:

If human rights are based on exclusively Eurocentric ideas, as many critics have (quite persistently) claimed, and these Eurocentric ideas are biased against non-Western countries and cultures, then the political legitimacy of human rights talk, human rights covenants, and human rights enforcement, is called into question.[11]

A society, for instance, that saw social role and context as pre-eminent in the definition of a person would be unlikely to be sympathetic to the idea of that person claiming rights that set one person apart from another. The Western love of individual autonomy would be regarded with suspicion. If it paid any attention to rights at all, it would be likely to give priority to economic and social ones in pursuit of what it saw as social justice. The prospect (and indeed the fact) of such basic international disagreement makes the issue of justification in terms of an overarching moral order only more pressing. We have to have a means, other than people's claims and aspirations, of validating, and even of demarcating, rights in the first place. Rights cannot depend on mere political agreements, when the will to recognize, and enforce, even the most basic ones is simply lacking. No doubt, rights can be made a matter of power, with powerful nations exerting their will. Even if they are driven themselves by a moral vision, the fact remains that they are imposing it on others merely through their power. Yet the point of an appeal to rights is that moral claims are introduced as an alternative to, and restraint on, the use of power. If rights become an instrument of power politics, the whole notion is negated.

A possible response to the idea that rights are the outcome of one culture is to say that their assertion is compatible with a moral pluralism that recognizes the existence of different moral perspectives. Perhaps human rights can rely simultaneously on many foundations. Ignatieff claims, for example, that a universal regime of human rights protection 'ought to be compatible with moral pluralism'.[12] There could be agreement on human rights, combined with disagreement about what constitutes a good human life. He says that 'people from different cultures may continue to disagree about what is good, but nevertheless agree about what is insufferably, unarguably wrong'. Such an overlapping consensus could be politically achievable, on the basis, perhaps, of a simultaneous appeal to the tenets of different religions, but an assertion of human rights must demand more than this. It involves claims to their objective validity everywhere, independent of how far they happen to be accepted in any given place.

As we shall see, 'pluralism', particularly in the context of morality, is always a slippery word. It can mean nothing more than the banal fact that there are different views and disagreements stemming from differences between different cultures and traditions. If it goes beyond this, it often suggests that there is no one right way of seeing things. No one could then adjudicate between alternative views, or suggest that any of them are in error. No one could have a monopoly possession of truth. This may appear to encourage toleration, but it does nothing to help the cause of human rights. We still have to face the unpalatable fact that not every regime will adopt the rhetoric of human rights, let alone recognize their existence. Amy Gutmann wants to advocate moral pluralism, but also admits that 'to say that a universal regime of human rights should be compatible with moral pluralism is not to say that it must be compatible with every belief system'.[13] Rights are, she believes, morally defensible in the face of oppressors who fail to recognize them.

Anyone who truly wishes to stand by the idea of rights must believe that they apply even when not recognized. This, though, is far from pluralism. A view of such rights that coexisted with a genuine pluralism would have to acknowledge that there were equally valid perspectives that rejected the notion. It is not possible to obtain the perceived benefits of pluralism – its toleration of other viewpoints and its refusal to be dogmatic – without the disadvantage of discovering that some viewpoints may be totally incompatible with one's own. We must either embrace the universal, objective, validity of human rights, or accept pluralism, and not apply standards to those who do not accept them. We might be able to forge political alliances when we can, and obtain some agreement about enforcing human rights. This, though, is a political issue, far removed from the moral high ground of asserting how humans ought to be treated because of a common humanity.

However much we may advocate moral truth, it is not enough simply to impose it on others, whether in an international context or within a particular society. As we have seen, a basic reason for the most basic rights is to protect our free agency. Morality and the freedom to choose are inseparable. There is, therefore, bound to be a tension between the provision of basic rights and the assumptions underlying them, between rights and freedom. The possession of rights by some may reduce the freedom of others. We have to ensure individual freedom, and respect it. This is particularly the case in a democracy where the wishes of the majority should not always be imposed on a minority. In crucial moral matters, my freedom of action should be preserved even if I am at odds with the majority. Similarly, there are some ways I should not be treated, even if a majority decide to do so. This inevitably produces problems for democratic politics, where a fear of the tyranny of the majority is not always misplaced. Arguments will break out about how far individual freedom should be preserved. Most would accept that I should not be coerced into accepting a religion I do not believe in. How far I should be expected to speak a language in public other than my native one is often a matter of controversy. Whether I can on conscientious grounds opt out of some of the duties of citizenship, such as the obligation to fight in defence of my country, is a fraught issue to which we shall return.

These are all problems even for a democratic society, and reflect the question of who should decide what rights there are, and how they should be specified. The issue is that such decisions should themselves be con- strained by the existence of basic rights. The decisions do not create the rights. Otherwise, a persecuted minority has no grounds for objecting because, by definition, the majority has decided which rights should exist. Like questions in international relations, talk of rights has to assume a prior web of moral claims to which international agreements, as well as domestic politics, should be subject. In other words, the objectivity and universality of human rights create a moral climate in which all decisions have to be made. Human beings are part of a moral order, which can be called 'natural' in so far as it is not the result of any definite human decision. If rights are constructed by agreement and convention, the very idea collapses into meaninglessness. It cannot be applied to those who reject it. Yet they are the people who should be most under judgement.

It is, of course, possible to reject the rhetoric of human rights. What one should not do is use it, trade on its claims to overriding truth yet not accept the implications that it carries about the objectivity of morals, and their intrinsic connections with our characteristics as human beings. Human rights belong in the moral sphere, and must be discussed as moral claims. They carry with them huge political and legal implications, but one cannot simply change the subject from morality to politics or law. Morality matters on its own. Without it, politics and law can be seriously cut adrift.

Notes

1   R. Hittinger, *The First Grace: Rediscovering the Natural Law in a Post-Christian World*, ISI Books, Wilmington, DE, 2003, p. 117.
2   Ibid., p. 130.

3 Michael Ignatieff, *Human Rights*, Princeton University Press, Princeton, NJ, 2001, p. 130.

4 Ibid., p. 108.

5 Ibid., p. 109.

6 Ibid.

7 Two Covenants, in *Mutilateral Treaty Framework: An Invitation to Universal Treaty Participation* (Johannesburg Summit), United Nations, New York, 2002, p. 2.

8 Ibid., p. 7.

9 Ibid.

10 Onora O'Neill, *A Question of Trust*, Cambridge University Press, Cambridge, 2002, p. 37.

11 Amy Gutmann, 'Introduction', in Ignatieff, *Human Rights*, p. xvii.

12 Ignatieff, *Human Rights*, p. 56.

13 Gutmann, 'Introduction', p. xx.

4

Natural rights and law

Can Laws Be Unjust?

We have seen how contemporary talk of human rights is rooted in a tradition going back to talk of natural rights in the seventeenth century. According to this view, morality has to be independent of 'positive' law, the enacted law of the land. In a well ordered society, indeed, it provides the underpinning and justification for law. Natural rights, as opposed to the rights of a citizen of a particular country, provide the framework in which law can be enacted. English common law developed over the centuries, building up a body of law out of a sense of justice and a desire for individual liberty. This heritage was in turn passed on, and further codified, in the Constitution of the United States of America. Any idea of natural rights is clearly closely connected with an idea of natural law. Both ideas relate views of how humans ought to be treated with issues about the way things are. It is not up to us, individually or collectively, to decide who is worthy of respect or not, and who should be treated with dignity. Indeed, it is not up to us to decide who is to be seen as of moral importance. That is, so natural law claims, ingrained in the nature of things.

A clear consequence of the belief in natural rights is the recognition that actual law can be unjust, because it ignores people's natural rights. In such circumstances, a corollary is that the people are justified in withdrawing their consent to be governed in that way. The philosopher John Locke himself had helped to finance the abortive 'Monmouth Rebellion', when the Duke of Monmouth had landed in 1685 in the west of England in an attempt to depose James II. The rebellion ended disastrously in the Battle of Sedgemoor in Somerset, but three years later Locke was on the boat with

Queen Mary sailing from Holland, when, in a bloodless change of monarchs, William and Mary acceded to the throne, and the Catholic King, James II, fled. Locke had rejected the laws of the time, on the ground that they were unjust, particularly in their restrictions on religious freedom. He gave a philosophical justification for revolution. The law cannot just rely on history and precedent, let alone the backing of mere power. It has to be just, recognizing what we now call human rights. Thus an English precedent was given for the later American Revolution, rejecting the authority of King George III. It was thought that respect for authority is not enough, since authority and power have themselves to be grounded in some higher authority, and linked to issues about our basic nature as human beings.

Perhaps such a vision gives too much encouragement to revolution, with all its dangers. Certainly the aftermath of both the French and Russian Revolutions was not unambiguously beneficial. Nevertheless, it robustly makes the case that laws themselves can be unjust, and that the whole system of law can be put on wrong foundations. One contemporary American writer says: 'The American law would begin by taking as profoundly serious the existence of the natural law, as the measure of the positive law, and the ultimate guarantor of a right to revolution.'[1] There were, in other words, substantive principles of justice, related to our role as human beings, which could be used to judge the justice of what is enacted in positive law. Justice ought to be reflected in the law of the land, although not defined by it.

Human rights, as an abstract concept, as opposed to their articulation within the principles of the common law, have not played much part in British law. The idea of natural law, as the foundation of positive law, has also been less visible in England than the United States. The issue has, however, never gone away. It is intriguing to note that in June 1953, in the issue of *The Times* of London reporting the Coronation the day before, one of the very few items not mentioning the Coronation was a letter from a retired judge. In it, he deplored 'the injury done to our juridical system by the disappearance of all recognition of the dependence of our national jurisprudence... on the natural law'. With the increasing emphasis in human rights in international and national politics, however, the issue cannot now be ignored. At first sight, at least, human rights have to be natural rights. It is anyway, as we have seen, now explicit that British law has to take account of such rights, whatever their basis. How far this will upset the traditional balance between Parliament and the courts remains to be seen, since enacted law will have to be subject to the demands of human rights. Judges will have considerable scope for interpretation of what precisely these may be in legal terms. The will of Parliament no longer appears to be the ultimate standard in law. Parliament's actions must now be open to legal scrutiny, and judged against some set of fairly abstract principles. It becomes increasingly vital that there be some understanding of where these principles come from, and what legitimates them. By definition, it is not the law of the land.

The Moral Background

Many of the most intractable problems in modern societies concern which rights carry most weight. Some want particularly to stress such rights as a right to choose and a right to privacy. The 'right to choose' is particularly relevant in issues about abortion, and a right to privacy in sexual matters, but these rights are much wider. They each share an emphasis on the pre-eminent role of the freedom of the individual, and a consequent desire to insulate individuals from public reproach. Individuals, it is thought, should be able to make their own decisions, and be protected from intrusion or criticism for what they do in private. Yet the paradox is that many want these rights to be publicly recognized and acted on. They want a public stance to be taken about their personal decisions and behaviour. They are not adopting a subjectivist ethics, according to which there can be no publicly agreed moral standards. The subjectivist believes that each decision is right for the individual making it. Those campaigning for any rights have to accept the need for public standards. It is just a question of what they should be. Appeals to rights to privacy and to freedom of choice may concentrate on the agency of the individual, but they appeal for public recognition.

There is a tension present in much modern debate. Those who claim rights to privacy and choice are often reluctant to see personal moral choices constrained by anything beyond the individual. They do not want to be told they could be mistaken, or that their choices should be judged against the demands of human nature. The very idea of rights, however, implies that we are dealing with issues that are not matters of individual decision. It cannot be up to me whether you have a right to privacy. Rights create claims on all of us, and cannot be acknowledged or repudiated as a matter of personal decision. Thus, rights to choose, and to privacy, may seem to reinforce a view of morality that leaves everything to the preferences, or tastes, of individuals. In fact they bring us face to face with all the demands of an objectivist ethics. So, far from ethics being private and individual, it has to be a public and social matter. That is why there is pressure for legal recognition of the claims being made. The issue, therefore, in such controversies is not whether there are 'natural' rights. The argument is which they are, and which have priority.

This issue of an objective morality carries with it implications about the way we regard human beings. We may accept that there can be 'objective' rights, belonging to humans, which demand recognition, even if they do not always receive it. Once we do this, however, it becomes clear that the idea of humanity must also have some objective moral weight. It follows that there is a fact of the matter about being human, and it is not a question of which society we happen to belong to. Arkes puts the matter this way:

> If there is no objective truth attaching to 'nature' or 'human nature', if the very meaning of a human being is, as some radical feminists say, always contingent, always open to 'contestation', then how could any of us be the bearers of rights that have objective standing? Could our rights, after all, have an objective standing, while we ourselves do not?[2]

This kind of question becomes particularly apposite when we are confronted by racism, or even slavery. Unless we can say that humans ought not to be treated in those ways, and appeal to the fact of our common humanity, we have a problem. Yet once it is conceded that 'humanity' is a social construction, so that what it means to be human depends on time and place, it can be easily argued that racism and slavery are the product of different social arrangements, which cannot be criticized by the standards of another society. There can then be no rational ground for challenging those standards. Only if it is recognized that the idea of human nature, and its status, is not the creation of any one society, and is not politically negotiable, will a society be judged by an objective criterion that holds, whatever those in power may happen to think. Power and truth need not coincide.

This suggests that law should not be merely a device to enable people to live together in a society. There are many ways of doing so, and some might make use of slavery. Even democratic agreement is not sufficient to make good law. That will depend on the vision of the world that is encoded in it. Locke, and the American Founders, were in no doubt that there could be unjust laws. Justice is not then constituted by the law, but should be reflected in it.

Two pictures of law are often contrasted. One is that of law encoding justice, and being constrained by rights. Positive law then reflects the natural law. Some might even see the courts as neutral arbiters of justice, in contrast to legislatures, which can be seen as the vehicles of competing special interests. There is, though, no reason why a conscientious legislator should not be as guided by morality as any judge. Conversely, judges themselves are not untouched by the political pressures put upon them. On the other hand, if the idea of a natural law is derided, we are left with positive law, as enacted in particular places. The law of the land must, it seems, be firmly under the democratic control of the representatives of the people. Law is then, it is claimed, the product of political negotiation. In pluralist societies, where there seems little agreement about many moral matters, democracy appears the only way of making decisions (although the plight of minorities remains an issue). Because of moral differences, it is often thought that the law should strive after moral neutrality. Individual freedom and mutual toleration are then usually extolled. Yet valuing freedom and toleration is not the mark of a neutral position. It involves advocating a specific kind of society, which happens to bear a marked resemblance to liberal democracy. Even laws providing a framework for that kind of society start from a vision of what is important about human beings. Not least, they stress the importance of the individual.

No law can ever be neutral from a moral point of view. The fact that something is allowed in a society sends a moral message, just as its prohibition does. Allowing freedom, even to make 'wrong' choices, gives the message of the importance of the idea of liberty. It is no coincidence that when people feel strongly, they are often not content with moral advocacy, but want their position to be given the force of law. This involves a level of compulsion, but many do not want to live in a society where certain things are tolerated. Those with strong views about animal cruelty do not just denounce fox hunting. They campaign for it to be outlawed.

The idea that law and morality are to be kept apart is a view that has grown with the insistence on individual autonomy. It is supposed that we should each choose how to live, within the limits of the need for a secure society. In that case, particular patterns of life should not be imposed by law. Freedom is everything. This liberalism, however, does not extend to basic questions about the kind of society that is being enforced. A liberal society is itself a particular kind of society buttressed by law. We have to accept that law is always a teacher. It shows people what is important enough to be prohibited. A law against spreading racial hatred, for instance, tells people what kind of behaviour is unacceptable. A right to free expression, on the other hand, if given the force of law, may take priority, and this, too, tells us about the moral priorities of a society. Arkes points out that legislation removes certain acts from the private domain, and this is inevitably to treat them as 'matters of moral consequence'. He says: 'As the public absorbs the understandings of right and wrong contained in the law, the character of the public becomes shaped for better or worse.'[3] Whatever messages are given by positive law, they have their effect. We may value liberty, or we may think certain things so dreadful they should be made illegal. Either way, we decide the kind of society we want to live in.

Yet law will still have its limitations from a moral point of view. Individual freedom and responsibility in moral matters must always transcend questions of legal accountability, not least because the functioning of law presupposes that moral basis. Obedience to the law is not enough, although it could be regarded as a moral obligation. We still have to make our own decisions about how to live, and how to treat others. Law can never anticipate all the complexities of human life, and if we are to be treated as free and responsible, it should not try to. It presupposes a pre-existing moral framework, and cannot create it.

Further, law cannot anticipate every possible situation, and make exact prescriptions, and so we often will have to rely on our own judgement. Indeed, this is an argument for giving judges some discretion in court as to the sentence they give. Legislatures often wish to tie their hands by laying down mandatory sanctions, and norms for sentencing may give useful guidelines to produce consistency across a jurisdiction. Nevertheless, even cases of murder differ, and no one can anticipate every type of mitigating factor. Moral discernment, governed by the circumstances of a particular case, is required in apportioning blame for actions, and deciding on a suitable punishment. Even in the trivial case of breaking a speed limit, there is a difference between a young man showing off in a sports car and an ambulance driver on a mercy mission.

The Law as Teacher

The administration of the law is the application of justice, and that is never morally neutral. Even small children have a deeply ingrained idea of what is not 'fair'. Elementary ideas of justice are so deeply rooted in us all that it appears that they answer to very basic human needs and impulses. Most people do not require any legal training to see that there is something wrong about being punished for something you have not done. Similarly, if you are found guilty of breaking a law passed some time after the act in question, most would agree that was highly unjust. Such human reactions are widespread, and it is at least arguable that they are not the simple product of social conditioning or education. They suggest a basic understanding of justice that springs from our very nature as human beings. Whether morality runs that deep is much contested. The more, however, that morality is thought to be a matter of social convention, and law is seen as merely expressing the arbitrary preferences of a particular society, the more each is devalued. Law matters because it is the public expression of morality. Yet if morality is made to appear arbitrary and relative, its importance and seriousness are thereby lessened.

Without morality, law could have little conception of what should be encouraged or discouraged. Like rules of the road, all law does have a regulatory function, but, without some conception of the purpose and aim of regulation, this can itself seem pointless. Even traffic laws are based on the presumption that human lives should be protected. Law, as we have seen, is a teacher. We have sometimes lost sight of this elementary fact, because we value individual freedom so much. We feel there should be a large space left for people to live their lives as they wish, without being subject to the compulsion of legal sanctions. Yet messages are sent by our decisions about what is important enough to be codified in law. There is always the danger that leaving something to individual decision makes it appear of less importance to society. It is hard, for instance, to consider that in the present age any civilized society would leave it to individual discretion as to whether to keep slaves. That is because a belief in the importance of human freedom has to extend to all humans. Yet this illustrates the point. Any society which values individual freedom, and human equality, is inevitably going to have a legal system based on those moral insights. It will be part of the social framework which is deliberately passed on through the generations.

Morality may often set higher standards than the law, in that it will expect moral agents to use their freedom in a responsible manner. This means that law alone is not going to be enough, although it will have its role in constraining our behaviour and showing us how best to act, and what to avoid. There must, in addition, be a place for moral education. If Aristotle was right in seeing the importance of habit in learning how to behave virtuously, it follows that children must be given training in how to behave, so that when they are adults, right behaviour comes naturally. This should be more than a matter of conditioning, but is essentially a rational process, so that we come to see why it is better to behave in some ways than others. From a liberal point of view, the very idea of moral training seems objectionable, and all too often moral education has appeared to avoid setting any standards. The stress on freedom has been taken to such lengths that it can seem as if the individual is to decide not just what it is best to do, but even what is to count as good or bad, right or wrong. In that situation, the very idea of the law as a moral guide is anathema. It could not be allowed to impose any particular idea of goodness, or any one vision of society.

The liberal position about law and morality has been well summarized as follows: 'Each citizen, it is affirmed, is the best judge of what is good for him or her: and government's job is to protect each citizen's right to frame his or her own choices about how to live, while avoiding the use of state power to favor particular choices or specific forms of life.'[4] The protection of individual choice is itself far from neutral as a moral position, and it involves the enforcement of specific rules and standards. Even if the object is to prevent interference in each other's affairs, that will imply constraints on people's behaviour. There will inevitably be clashes when a desire to uphold toleration meets moral positions which demand that certain practices be outlawed. A tolerant society cannot both respect individual decisions in sexual matters and uphold everyone's right to their own views about what kind of society we should live in. Many wish not just to hold private beliefs about, say, the immorality of abortion or homosexuality, but to live in a society which sets the same standards as they themselves have. Yet that would not be a 'liberal' society, and for the liberal it cannot even be discussed as an option. The change from a society that tolerates particular actions to one that outlaws them, like the change from restriction to toleration, is not an interchange between a specific moral outlook and a studied independence of all such outlooks. It is simply itself a moral change, involving a different ordering of priorities. This is not an argument against liberalism. It merely points out that the liberal idea that the law does not legislate about morals is an illusion. The legal requirement for toleration involves a specific moral stance. It is undeniable that as laws about homosexuality have changed, so have attitudes in society.

Whenever any behaviour is deliberately removed from the attention of the law, a strong message is sent to society. Individual freedom is being valued more, for example, than the content of some people's moral opinions. Whether this is good or bad is not the point. Changing the law does not leave everything as it was, but will lead to a change in behaviour. This is a point often made in arguments about the liberalization of laws on drugs. The mere fact of changing a law on, say, selling heroin would itself positively encourage a change in behaviour. The restraint of law, and of public opinion expressed through the law, would be decisively removed. In addition, whether this would be intended or not, the message would be given that the attitude of society had changed, and that it no longer saw some things as unequivocally wrong. The tightening of laws on smoking in public places shows the working of law in the opposite direction. What was previously socially acceptable has now become less so, and this inevitably becomes reflected in public regulations.

Liberalism and the Law

How far can moral views be imposed on those who do not voluntarily accept them? Law is a means of doing so, and it raises large issues in a free society. Nowhere is this more the case than where legislation is intended for people's own good. All legislation constrains us, and so we have to recognize that some restrictions are inevitable. Rules of the road may limit our freedom, but everyone will accept their necessity, if we want to stay alive. What is always contested, however, is whether the law may make me do something in my interest, when I do not want to, and it will not harm anyone else. For example, should everyone be made to wear seat belts, or stopped from smoking? There appears to be no one answer to this type of question. It may well depend on circumstances. Presumably individual freedom, while valuable, is not the only thing that is important. A liberal society may value it to the exclusion of everything else, but this itself is to come to a specific moral conclusion. More paternalistic views may wish, on occasion, to protect people from themselves. While not a currently fashion-able view, it is not obvious that it is always wrong.

One powerful reason for not letting the law be an arbiter between differ-ences in moral outlook is the fact of moral disagreement. This becomes more significant when the conviction weakens that moral issues have any concern with truth. The idea that citizens are the best judges of what is good for themselves comes very close to the idea that there is no objective standard of goodness anyway. Moral outlooks then seem like differences of taste: I may dislike bananas, and you may disapprove of abortion. Both attitudes tell something about us, and not the kind of society we should have. Yet a creeping subjectivism, making truth in moral matters merely truth 'for someone', sits uneasily with a liberal outlook. Beliefs in human equality and individual liberty are themselves substantive moral beliefs. People have literally fought to set up societies based on them. The French Revolution struggled to obtain *liberté*, *égalité* and *fraternité*, and those words are still inscribed on the front of the Palais de Justice in Paris. Such principles cannot be left to individual decision as to whether they should be accepted, any more than justice is just a product of individual taste.

Liberalism may at times appear to encourage subjectivism, but in fact it must itself be destroyed by it. Relegating matters to private decision may be done out of a deep respect for the individual. Yet saying that they should not be of any concern to law can be understood as saying that they are not important enough for a public position to be taken. Individual liberty is to take absolute precedence. This may point to the kind of society people want to have, but it should be a matter for moral debate. Leaving some matters to individual decision, away from the public arena, has the effect of prohibiting public debate on the morality of some issues. What are allowed as 'public reasons' come to be of a very specific kind, and moral issues can even be excluded on the grounds that they are private. This may be partly because of a fear that moral questions can be entangled with religious ones, but it is not obvious that a public debate about religion is harmful.

Many may still be unhappy about legislating about moral questions, even if they fully accept that moral issues are concerned with truth. They might feel that there is something questionable about compelling people to be good. Genuine morality surely arises out of free choice, not compulsion. Law, too, it may be said, is ill-advised in interfering with what is properly private. That is a different point from distinction between subjectivity and objectivity. Law, of its nature, makes public prescriptions and has to be publicly enforced. Much private behaviour may be beyond its reach, simply because of difficulties in enforcing the law in such circumstances. Unenforceable law is always bad law. Many, too, may feel uncomfortable if the law encourages, literally or metaphorically, spying through keyholes. Modern technology gives much greater scope for this. Yet the dichotomy between public and private is always going to be somewhat artificial. Many private actions have public consequences, and the law has to take account of them. A murder is not less criminal when committed in conditions of utmost privacy.

Law and morality can never be coextensive. People cannot be made to be good, but the law can create conditions in which it is easier or more difficult for them to become so. When they are forced to refrain from certain actions, they are not thereby virtuous, or acting from the best of motives. Law itself needs a pre-existing moral foundation. Its nature depends on the morality of legislators, and its effectiveness on the morality of citizens who regard it as a duty to obey it. A law that cannot count on obedience by most people, simply because it is the law, but depends wholly on the threat of sanctions and the fact of enforcement, rests on a very insubstantial foundation. Corrupt legislators, like unjust judges and dishonest police, themselves undermine the rule of law. The latter depends on a prior framework of morality. Virtue precedes law, and cannot be created by it.

Hadley Arkes refers to, as he puts it, 'the cliché, gleaned so widely these days from sociology and fortune cookies, that we must never "legislate morality"'.[5] He claims that we should say that 'we may legislate only morality'. That seems startling at first to those schooled in the principles of liberalism, and appears to be suggesting that we can make people moral. Yet what has to be the case is that the law cannot ignore the demands of morality. All law should be based on moral principle. We should be very suspicious of it when it is being made with any other motivations; for instance, to serve particular commercial interests. Law operating in a moral vacuum – or, worse, based on injustice – cannot command the assent and obedience of those citizens who are expected to comply with it.

Law has to be respected, if it is not merely to be obeyed out of fear. In a democratic society, it cannot be imposed arbitrarily, but needs the agreement of those it will affect. Everyone's interests have to be taken into account, and not just those of a particular section of a society. This is a question of how we should live together and respect each other. It is a typical moral question. Law has to be based on morality, and decisions about the nature and scope of the law have to depend on a deep moral sensitivity. Morality itself also needs law. Some of our central concerns as humans have to be given concrete expression in a way that sets standards for a society. Yet law has to be our servant, not our master. Without morality, it can be dangerous and arbitrary. Without the force of law, morality itself can be ineffective.

Should the Law Allow Torture?

Article 5 of the United Nations Declaration of Human Rights proclaims that 'no one shall be subjected to torture or to cruel, inhuman or degrading treatment or punishment'. This is thought to follow from our basic character as human beings, each of which is the bearer of a dignity that should be respected. The United Nations presumably expects such a right not just to be enshrined in an international law whose status is still vague, but also to be codified in the laws of member countries. Torture should be universally illegal. Law, it seems, should prohibit what, according to morality, undermines our position as free and responsible agents. Certainly if law is to articulate any kind of moral view, it is hard to imagine how it could allow torture.

What, though, is wrong with torture? By definition, it involves the deliberate infliction of suffering, of something a person does not want. Not all need be directly physical. It is perfectly possible to torture someone by threatening the safety of their family, and even by inflicting suffering on them in front of that person. The purpose of torture, however, is to make a person care for nothing more than the cessation of the suffering. Its purpose is to break down someone's autonomy and reason, by manipulating them in a dehumanizing manner. The cruelty is bad enough, but, like slavery, its function is the reverse of respecting anyone's humanity. It is, to use Kant's famous terminology, to treat someone as a means and not as an end.

Some, though, may convince themselves that information to be gained from a captured terrorist may be so vital that even respect for human life might make us resort to any means to obtain it, so as to save lives. Utilitarian calculations about consequences may come into play. We may start balancing one person's undoubted suffering against the prospect of saving many lives. Perhaps we can prevent a major terrorist attack. Even democratic states are accused of being willing to torture in such circumstances. There will, too, always be an argument, sometimes self-serving, over what constitutes 'torture' or 'inhumane' treatment. Deliberate and prolonged deprivation of sleep may be different from more direct physical methods, but its effect can be devastating. Nevertheless, whatever the method, the weighing of costs and benefits will lead some to agree with the American lawyer Alan M. Dershowitz when he says: 'It is surely better to inflict non-lethal pain on one guilty terrorist who is illegally withholding information needed to prevent an act of terrorism than to permit a large number of innocent victims to die.'[6] As with all utilitarian calculations, matters are not usually that stark. We normally only deal with suspicions and risks. Part of the problem is that we cannot usually be certain of guilt if we do not have all the information. If we did have it, we would not be tempted to resort to torture.

No one who has to deal with dangerous and desperate people will imagine that truth can be obtained by polite questions and answers over a cup of tea. Pressure of some kind may have to be applied if the interrogators are not themselves to be merely dismissed with contempt. The question, though, is what kind and how much. One problem is that excessive pressure may obtain answers, but not the truth. Someone who is sufficiently demoralized may become anxious to say what the tormentors want to hear. The only motive will be to remove the pressure by saying anything. It is easy to extract a confession of 'guilt' by being ruthless, but even the innocent may then be prepared to give one. The very process of dehumanization is one which quickly obliterates any distinction between truth and falsity. All that matters is what will stop the torture.

It is, however, possible to construct hypothetical scenarios where a terrorist knows the location of a nuclear bomb, and has to be made to divulge it, so as to save a city. One suggestion that has been seriously made by Dershowitz is that any such torture should be preceded by a 'torture warrant' granted by a judge. His argument is that 'a formal, visible, accountable, and centralized system is somewhat easier to control than an *ad hoc*, off-the-books, and under-the-radar-screen non-system'.[7] This procedure might appear to regularize a situation that is going to occur anyway. Instead of pursuing a policy of silence and pretence, the state faces up to the fact that torture may be necessary as an instrument of policy. It thus gives judges, as neutral observers, the right to decide in what circumstances this can by allowed by law. This will supposedly prevent an abuse of the system. Yet it immediately makes the law acknowledge, and even approve of, a practice that most would consider should be absolutely ruled out on all occasions. That is the point of the UN Declaration. Can law entertain something that morality rules out absolutely? A utilitarian might reply that nothing can be ruled out in that way, as the consequences of doing so in a particular situation might be worse than not doing so.

Many, however, will feel that the legitimation of torture in *any* circumstances already constitutes a major abuse of the rule of law. Moreover, if the law of a land allows torture, that will be going against the very natural law that gives law its point. There are some things that law can never countenance. Many would say that all killing should equally be prohibited, and would rule out capital punishment. Certainly assassination, as an instrument of policy, would seem to be hard to justify. Utilitarians could produce arguments about the benefits of ridding the world of a dangerous dictator, but it is hard to see how any legal system could explicitly allow for it. The act would be murder, even if the circumstances might provide mitigation, and suggest a lenient punishment. Yet Dershowitz is also prepared to countenance 'targeted assassination' as a means of dealing with terrorists, and argues for its official authorization 'in extreme cases where the threat is great, the certainty high, and the unavailability of other mechanisms of incapacitation certain'.[8] The problem will always be that once an absolute prohibition in law is qualified, a slippery slope leads us to tolerate more and more exceptions. A readiness to torture leads on to a willingness to assassinate, and that leads on to an ever greater use of questionable means to achieve what is regarded as a just end. In the end, defenders of liberty and justice can become indistinguishable from the dictators they confront.

Allowing the legal regulation of torture countenances what should never be countenanced. If desperate circumstances lead people to torture, they are still acting immorally and against the law, even if there may be mitigating factors. What kind of judges would even be willing to allow torture (particularly if they then had to act as observers)? Presumably many would resign rather than administer a law allowing such actions. It is hardly reassuring that one would be left with those who have no great compunction about underwriting cruelty. This indicates how torture cannot be separated from wider views about the worth of human beings and how they ought to be treated. A person, or a system of law, that regards people as expendable for the greater good may be operating according to strict utilitarian principles. Nevertheless, once injustice is accepted as an explicit and integral part of policy, a precedent is created. Regimes that openly practise torture are usually also guilty of wider injustice and oppression.

Only a principled stand against all injustice can preserve the integrity of law as an instrument for the protection of the innocent, and for the delivery of justice. Once positive law and justice become parted, the moral force of law is weakened. It becomes the tool of the state, to be used in arbitrary ways. It is no longer the stern protector of the rights of those it is supposed to protect. Law cannot be compromised by codifying unjust actions. Those who may be driven in extreme situations to torture or kill should still be answerable for their actions in a court of law, whatever mitigation might be offered. Law cannot be compromised, and its connection with basic moral principle must remain intact. Morality and law are far from identical, but all law depends on moral authority to be obeyed. Once it becomes a mere instrument of power, its efficiency will be strictly proportionate to the power of those in a position to enforce it. Totalitarian methods are inevitable once a respect for the rule of law, rooted in morality, is removed. All that is then left is power.

Notes

1 Hadley Arkes, *Natural Rights and the Right to Choose*, Cambridge University Press, Cambridge, 2002, p. 12.
2 Ibid., p. 181.
3 Ibid., p. 3.
4 Peter Berkowitz, *Virtue and the Making of Modern Liberalism*, Princeton University Press, Princeton, NJ, 1999, p. x.
5 Hadley Arkes, *First Things: An Inquiry into the First Principles of Morals and Justice*, Princeton University Press, Princeton, NJ, 1980, p. 27.
6 A. M. Dershowitz, *Why Terrorism Works: Understanding the Threat, Responding to Its Challenge*, Yale University Press, New Haven, CT, 2002, p. 144.
7 Ibid., p. 152.
8 Ibid., p. 184.

5

The rule of law

What Is the Difference between Moral Rules and Laws?

Law and morality may be intertwined, but we have seen that they are definitely distinct. Do they function, though, in parallel ways, or are they very unlike each other? Are moral rules in any way like the laws of a land? A crucial difference is that, if such rules have a claim to objective truth, and are related to human nature, they must have a universal application. Laws are local. The laws of England do not apply in the United States, and vice versa, even though they may be derived from the same principles. This distinction fails to operate for a relativist, for whom morality is itself local and conventional. The only distinction, then, between moral and legal rules is that the sanctions for breaking the law are codified. There may be shame or reproach when we flout convention, but there are no clearly agreed punishments in the same way.

Many would object to any idea of morality being conveyed in a set of rules, to be applied on particular occasions like law. Yet morality cannot be allowed to dissolve into a morass of private decisions, which may ultimately be arbitrary. There has to be a set of standards or principles which apply to my actions, whether or not I happen to abide by them at any one time. The relativist might point to the publicly enforced conventions and habits of society, and we are then not far from the analogy with the law of a particular place. Even in ancient Greece, there were major arguments between those who traced morality to law and custom, the *nomos* of a particular place, and those who looked to a universal grounding in nature, *physis*, which by definition was the same everywhere.

Can moral principle, even so, be compared in some ways with law? In the case of law itself, there is a difference between the principles underlying it and actual laws. Sometimes such principles are enshrined in a constitution. The presumption in favour of free speech is, for instance, spelt out in the First Amendment of the Constitution of the United States. Yet even the American Constitution, as we have seen, depends on more basic principles concerning the natural equality of 'all men'. This reflects the idea that law ought to be obeyed because it reflects a basic moral vision of the world. To say that the law is the law because it is the law, and has no further justification, is itself to push us to moral relativism. Acceptance by a society will then constitute the reality both of law and of morality for that society.

There is an obvious merit in having a set of laws known to everyone in order to guide behaviour. We know what is expected of us, and what to expect of others. Everyone can then depend on each other, since we will live in a human world that is broadly predictable. When we know which side of the road everyone is driving on, we can do the same and not have any nasty surprises round corners. Rules in morality, at the very least, carry those advantages.

William Galston juxtaposes two different notions about legal judgement. We could adhere strictly to rules without exception, or we could adopt an 'equity-based' jurisprudence, which only looks at the facts of each case. There are analogues with ethical positions. A strict adherence to rules, come what may, can be contrasted with views (such as situation ethics and act utilitarianism) according to which moral decisions should be taken only in the light of a particular context. As Galston writes: 'The problem with strict rules is that they will inevitably run up against exceptional cases, in which their application will appear harsh and unreasonable. The problem with unfettered equity is that it requires little predictability or uniformity, diluting the principal advantages of the rule of law.'[1]

A rule of law is often regarded as a mark of any free society. There is a seeming paradox here, in that freedom and constraint would seem opposed, and law is, after all, in the business of constraint. Yet freedom demands stability. Law provides a framework in which individuals can lead their lives as they wish, in security and freedom from fear. A lack of law as a guide, with a mere appeal to abstract principles, will fail to provide that framework. Law has to be public, since laws must be widely understood in order to be obeyed. Its nature is closely linked with fairness and consistency of application. People cannot live according to a rule of law that is arbitrary or inconsistent, that involves the malevolent exercise of power or that submerges the principles animating the law in a welter of bureaucratic detail. An unprincipled exercise of law, which lays aside issues of justice and equity, crushes citizens rather than providing the framework in which they are free to lead their own lives.

For these reasons, the retrospective application of laws is unfair and unjust. Law should guide actions so that citizens can live together. Even a community of perfect beings, who were not tempted to take advantage of each other, would still need guidelines. Laws that have a retrospective effect clearly fail this elementary purpose of law. Making any law reach back to include those who could not have adjusted their actions to take account of it undermines, rather than strengthens, the rule of law. It is unjust even to legislate retrospectively against great moral wrongs, merely because of their evil. We might condemn the perpetrators, but the point of an introduction of a law would be to give them the opportunity to change their ways.

The nature of public law is that it is codified, and should not be left to some private understanding of equity or justice on the part of magistrates or judges. Yet Galston's point that strict rules have sometimes to be modified in the face of exceptions must always be a problem. We shall return to it in the case of moral rules, which can sometimes clash. Galston wants to argue for 'the jurisprudence of presumptions', which, he says, 'emerges as an attempt to combine the advantages of rules – clarity, predictability, uniformity – with those of flexibility, prudence and common sense'.[2] Legal presumptions can be rooted in the rule of law, while it is recognized that no law can anticipate every precise circumstance to which it may be applicable. There should, therefore, never be any exceptionless, absolute principles in law. Galston says that 'those that may appear absolute are in fact strong presumptions that may be overcome in specific circumstances'.[3]

There is in this an alleged parallel between law and morality. Galston argues: 'Like legal rules, moral and political principles act on rebuttable presumptions. . . . No principle is absolute, that is exceptionless.'[4] We shall later query this as an account of moral principles, but problems also arise with law. Laws which are properly laid down and promulgated should not easily be set aside. Given the facts in a particular case, it may become clear that a law does not apply. That means the person was not guilty in the first place of breaking it. A person accused of shoplifting may in fact have paid for the goods. Galston, however, appears to consider that exceptions can be made even if the law does appear to apply. Each case has to be heard on its merits, since each context differs, but that does not mean that the law should not apply. Even shoplifting could occur in a context where one might have reason for sympathizing with the defendant, or see that the person needs help. Yet that cannot alter the question of guilt according to the law. It merely raises the question of the appropriate punishment, if any.

The administration of law has to take place with sensitivity and compassion, but it is the law that is being administered, and not the personal judgements of the magistrates or judge. The rule of law demands that it cannot be relegated to the status of mere presumption, any more than the moral principles underlying it can be. If a law is to be set aside in the interests of equity, is the principle of equity to be set aside when the demands of state are pressing? This does nothing to cast doubt on the fact that each case will vary, and due regard must be given to its own particular circumstances. Punishments will vary, and it might not even be appropriate to give one. Someone in England can be given an absolute discharge if the circumstances warrant. They may be comparatively blameless in having broken the law, but it is recognized that they did break it. They may have broken a speed limit which was not clearly marked. The law applies, but the facts are taken into account. That is not the same as saying the law does not apply.

Judicial Activism

The issue of judicial discretion raises the question of the function of judges at the highest level. In the United States the Supreme Court has to interpret the Constitution, and it can do so in a way that runs counter to the will of Congress. Once there is a written constitution, which lays down basic rights for citizens, laws can easily be passed that allegedly run counter to the proper exercise of those rights. Indeed, such constitutional guarantees are precisely intended to protect citizens against oppressive law. The tug between Congress and the Supreme Court is a familiar one in the United States, but increasingly it is becoming a familiar situation elsewhere. The European Union is progressively laying down rights enshrined constitutionally for its citizens, in ways that must inevitably challenge the authority of national parliaments. Even from a totally international standpoint, the advent of the International Criminal Court provides the possibility of accusations being brought about abuses of human rights even against democratically elected politicians.

Who should have the final say about rights in a democratic country? Should Parliament or Congress be able to represent the will of the people, however imperfectly, or should rights be safeguarded by the supposedly dispassionate and neutral judgements of courts? This might appear to be a political question about power, but it raises the deepest issues of principle. Once one accepts that the rights of individuals have to be protected, the temptation is to assume that those rights cannot simply be subject to a popular vote. They do not depend on majority opinion. It seems that there ought to be a mechanism by which rights can be safeguarded without being at the mercy of shifting political alliances or power struggles. Even well intentioned politicians might be ready to sacrifice a few in the interests of the many. Utilitarians have always been suspicious of talk of rights, since they provide firm obstacles in the way of those who make calculations about the general good.

Once, though, rights are protected by the courts, the power of politicians is necessarily circumscribed. Legislation can be struck down. Many have a cynical view of politicians and think this a good idea, but they may also have an unduly optimistic view of the capabilities, rationality and even political neutrality of even the most able judges. The problem is not, though, who is more trustworthy. That might vary from time to time. The issue is who in principle has the right to decide how society should be organized. A belief in natural law might appear to encourage giving power to judges, so that they can judge according to its principles. Such natural law is supposed to be accessible to reason, and not political calculation. Yet even given that positive law can be unjust, the problem is still who should decide that, and put matters right. Why should judges alone have the capacity to make rational decisions about what is morally required? Do they have an insight into the moral basis of society denied others? There might be major objections if such issues were to be decided by a panel of bishops. Why should a bench of judges be in any different position? They are likely to be of a particular age and come from a definite section of the intelligentsia. Perhaps they will merely exhibit the prejudices of their time and place.

Many are certainly concerned about the expansion of judicial power, and the so-called judicial activism that it implies. Robert George refers to theorists such as Ronald Dworkin, who argue that judges must call on moral and political philosophy in hard cases. He contrasts this with those, such as Judge Robert Bork, who, as he says, 'fear such a role for the judge, and hold, that in any event the Constitution of the United States does not give the judge such a role'.[5] This, though, is not a parochial American argument. The issue is how far judges should appeal to objective standards of justice, and deep issues of principle, or whether they should be constrained by the particular laws pertaining to their jurisdiction. It is a problem that arises in different ways in any country. Judges might wish to resist a tyrannical regime. At the same time, in a democracy, many might consider that they should defer to the representatives of the people.

One may hope that a natural law, if there is one, would not be contradicted, but if a democratic legislature makes a definite decision that appears to transgress it, the issue is whether judges have the right to strike the law down? One only has to look at arguments about abortion to see how crucial it is whether courts or legislature have the final say. Even if all parties were to agree that there is a natural law, who is to decide, in a contentious case like that, what the natural law demands? If one thinks of natural rights, are those of the mother or the unborn child to be given priority? Someone has to decide the law in such cases, and courts and lawmakers may not come to the same conclusion.

The Role of Judges

Even if it were accepted that positive law does not exist in a vacuum, but gains much of its force by reflecting an underlying moral order, the question still remains. Who is to decide not just what is right and wrong, but how far such judgements should be publicly enforced? Judges are professionally supposed to be impartial, but they are no less susceptible to prejudice than the rest of us. Some may have a religious, or anti-religious, axe to grind. Many (particularly in some countries) may owe their appointments to political influence, and perhaps are even expected to pursue a political agenda. It is perhaps too much to hope that they will be able to function like Plato's philosopher-kings, able to discern infallibly what is just, and then implement it. A legislature, Parliament, Congress or whatever, can claim to be at least more directly representative of the will of the people. Its members, in a democracy, will have been elected, and are accountable to their electors. They will not be re-elected if they outrage the moral beliefs of those they purport to represent.

A belief in natural law, and the relevance of reason to morality, need not inevitably lead to giving judges priority over lawmakers. They may not be any more likely to see its force than those who are responsive to public opinion. It is a notable form of elitism, and distrust of democracy, which can suppose that judges are to be trusted, and politicians not. The ground for believing this is that judges can, it is hoped, be independent of political pressures. In other words, what ordinary people think does not matter. Yet anyone who believes in democracy, and in the common sense of ordinary people, may hesitate about handing over major decisions about the shape of our society to a small group, who themselves are part of an intellectual elite.

Pornography, for example, might seem to judges to be the regrettable but inevitable result of a right to free expression, which must not be curtailed. Yet ordinary voters may be affronted by what is available on their television screens and elsewhere. If judges, alone, have the power to decide what if any censorship at all can be justified, the result may be a gradual transformation of a society. 'Free expression' can be extended to include such things as nude dancing (though it may not be entirely clear what such dancing is intended to express). What was once regarded as unacceptable in public entertainment becomes normal. Yet it may still occur against the wishes of the majority of citizens. The law is made into a vehicle of social change, merely because of how it is interpreted by judges. There need then be no democratic discussion about its desirability.

The issue of whether interpretation of natural law should be left to judges has nothing to do with natural law itself. The ability of judges to make new law is a different issue from whether positive law should rest on some foundation. Even given natural law, there may be a lot to be said for restricting the powers of judges. Judicial appeal to abstract principle, so that judges venture beyond what has been laid down by statute, and interpreted by case law, may seem downright dangerous. It gives judges the apparent right to range beyond existing law, and can suddenly alter a whole legal framework, without public discussion or consultation. As a result it challenges the ability of any elected government to govern effectively. In Britain, the sovereignty of Parliament has always been considered of supreme importance. Once a parliament is subordinated to any other institution, the ability of a people to govern itself democratically is undermined. The institutions of the European Union are seen by some as a threat to British democracy. Certainly the doctrine of the sovereignty of Parliament will have to be modified as those institutions gain in authority. In a similar fashion, such sovereignty is challenged if judges are given the opportunity to overturn specific legislation in the name of 'human rights', 'natural law' or some such notion.

There is nothing to stop a country deciding to entrust its judges with the responsibility of interpreting the natural law, and holding positive law accountable to it. 'Human rights', for instance, can be delineated in a charter of rights, and judges can be entrusted with sorting out their practical application, using their own moral judgement. That, though, depends on the particular constitution of a country. The point is that judicial power is itself to be circumscribed by enacted law. Once judges start relying on 'justice', regardless of what the law says, they may be exceeding their powers. Robert George sums up the matter well when he says in an American context: 'To the extent that judges are not given power under the Constitution to translate principles of natural justice into positive law, that power is not one they enjoy, nor is one they may justly exercise.'[6] It is a paradox indeed that, by pursuing justice (or their own idea of it) regardless of their powers, they themselves are transgressing a basic principle of justice. They should not misuse their own powers. The responsibility of any judge is to administer particular laws, and their own function is set out by law. They should not extend their role, so as to challenge the same legal basis which gives them a right to adjudicate.

A belief in natural law suggests that such law must be accessible to reason, and it is accessible to everyone. Natural law claims universality, and it is not something vouchsafed to an intellectual elite, but not to others who wish to reason in an informed manner. There is no reason at all why the principles of natural law, if such there be, can only be ascertained by the Supreme Court, or the Law Lords, but not to members of Congress or Parliament, or ordinary electors. Expertise in the law does not inevitably carry with it great moral insight. Judges are certainly sometimes tempted to extend the scope of appeals to rights in ways that may not always be obvious.

A measure to limit campaign financing might be passed by the United States Congress, and then blocked by the Supreme Court on the grounds that it limits freedom of speech. Yet it is arguable that the need for an excessive amount of money to finance political campaigns is ultimately corrupting and anti-democratic. Stopping money being given to support a candidate might seem an assault on freedom, but so might the effective restriction of election to those with access to wealthy backers. The issue is not who is right, but whether the matter should be decided by judges or by representatives of the people. However cynical a view may be held about politicians, it remains clear that the more decisions are left to the courts, the less democratic control is left. Even if the courts were more likely to make sound judgements than politicians, there still remains the question of whether the production of a properly ordered society, controlled by an elite, is preferable to a society where citizens have some measure of influence themselves over how they should be governed.

The idea that law must have a moral basis goes against the kind of contract theory that sees law as the product of individuals coming together for mutual protection. We thus band together and have laws out of self-interest, in contrast with the lack of security of a 'state of nature', as Thomas Hobbes understood it. There must indeed be some connection between law and individual interest, since law must have a connection with what is good for humans if it is to be genuinely just, and to reflect a moral understanding. It is, however, a grave mistake to think that keeping the law will always be in one's interest, and making that connection may make it appear rational on occasion to break the law. Why should someone keep an agreement, or abide by a contract, if it might be more convenient to break it (particularly if one could do so without being detected)? This question will always arise if one does not see the moral basis of society and of the law constituting it. It will arise if morality and the pursuit of self-interest are somehow conflated. The only solution is to see the moral force of law, and to accept a moral obligation to obey the law simply because it is the law, as long, at least, as it is attempting to articulate justice.

A deeply fractured society is in trouble when it cannot obtain agreement about what constitutes good and harm, and what the law should encourage and what it should discourage. Liberal ideas are often taken up in such a situation, with the idea that the law can somehow be a neutral regulator. In addition, some distinction is made between public and private, with the aim of keeping public law away from the latter. As we have already seen, any law-governed society needs a morality that is more than personal choice, arbitrary commitment or the pursuit of individual advantage. No legal system can survive if citizens think that they can pick and choose which laws to keep. No such system can be neutral about whether it ought to be obeyed or not. People must be willing to be law-abiding as a matter of moral principle. Membership of a society carries with it obligations and responsibilities that precede law and are not created by it.

The impartiality demanded of magistrates and judges is itself a moral demand. Yet just because of the close connection between law and morality, there are dangers here. What of those who may not share a moral vision enshrined in law? The necessity to respect that individual freedom which is the mainspring of morality should make us wary of allowing the views of one section of society to be imposed on another. Just because of the link between morality and law, the function of law should always be to enhance and safeguard moral responsibility, not to undermine it by taking away our freedom to make moral choices. If law is really to reflect morality, it should also foster its basis, namely freedom of conscience. Unless we can of our own accord see what we ought to do, we can never be the kind of moral agent needed to uphold law. The need for toleration and mutual respect follows from this, but clearly has its limits. Many would still not wish to live in the kind of society which allowed certain things they opposed. Nevertheless, we should be wary of imposing a moral conformity through law. Once the law itself provokes dissent, and encourages people to break it on moral grounds, the rule of law is in danger.

A certain level of disagreement seems to follow from the nature of democracy, at least given human nature. In a perfect world we might all be able to agree, but in this world rational argument and discussion thrive on varying views, given human fallibility. Democracy itself has its own moral justification, by taking seriously the moral responsibility of each citizen, and their right (and duty) to participate in the forming of policy. It does not rely on being a majority option, but rests on a belief in the natural equality of all. Humans are able to understand, and discuss, through their rationality, justifications for action and policy in a way that even the most intelligent animals cannot. They can take responsibility for what they decide. This is a fact of human nature, holding for rich and poor, male and female, and all races. Hadley Arkes is quite explicit in making democracy depend on natural law, saying that 'the rightness of government by consent is simply rooted in nature, in the things that make human beings different from animals'.[7] We cannot change that nature, but have to live in accordance with it.

The idea that any particular form of government should be dependent on natural law may appear bold, particularly given the many varieties there have been, and are. Yet any constitutional arrangement cannot ignore basic facts of human nature, and it must take seriously the natural equality of human beings. There may still be arguments as to what grounds that equality, and why human nature is as it is. Any system, however, which treats people differently on arbitrary grounds, such as wealth or social standing, is challenging a most basic feature of humanity. The claim to equality is the moral one that everyone ought to be treated by the same standards. Justice cannot be local, or particular, in its application. That in turn implies an important fact about the law in a free society. Everyone is equal before it, and no one can properly claim privileges if they break it.

Arkes defines an idea of constitutional government, a government by law, as 'republican'. Its first maxim, he claims, is that 'people in positions of authority should be compelled to cite some law beyond their own self-interest as the ground of their official acts'[8] The restraint of law on those in government, and its impartiality, provides a bulwark against the arbitrary use of power, enabling individuals to regulate their lives in a way that is free from the fear of being seized and punished in a random fashion. It is easy to take this for granted, but it is the most precious and indispensable element of a free society. The use of the term 'republican' is unfortunate, in that it may suggest that any monarchy is incompatible with it. That may be an American view. Nevertheless, while a monarch, unrestrained by law, is as much a threat to the ideal of impartial, constitutional government as any other tyrant or dictator, constitutional monarchy is itself an exemplification of it. The Crown, as the symbol of fair and impartial government, and the guarantor of the independence of the judiciary, can be a potent instrument for the rule of law. The monarch can, thanks to the history of a particular nation, become the literal embodiment of constitutional government, acting in accordance with custom and tradition to guarantee the basic principles of law.

Conscientious Objectors

It is all very well talking of the rule of law, and of disagreement in a democracy. What happens when a law is duly passed, and a minority find that they cannot on moral grounds accept it? People's moral views should be respected, but no society, it seems, can tolerate its citizens simply opting out of it. We all wish not to pay taxes, if we disapprove of government policy (and perhaps even if we do not). Yet any society, however democratic, would soon break down if its decisions were not collectively enforced. In a civilized society it is recognized that a balance has to be struck. There are some things, it seems, people should not be forced to do against their conscience, such as fighting in a war. Pacifists, such as those in the Society of Friends, have long been able to obtain exemption from fighting, although they then served in other ways, perhaps in an ambulance service. Thus conscientious objectors are not 'free-riders' benefiting while not contributing. This is important, as many might well resent it if some members of a society had to take risks, and even die, while another section is spared danger.

There may still be an argument about not giving exemptions to conscientious objectors. We are faced with people who are making a moral judgement about war. If they are right, it follows that we should not be fighting in the first place. How can we respect their judgement once we consider that we can do no other than fight in the circumstances? What does such respect amount to, if we consider that war, however evil, is not the worst available choice? We certainly cannot think that the objectors are more justified, or more worthy of esteem, than the rest of us, since we think they are mistaken. We cannot even think they are more morally sensitive, since that again is to admit that they are right. If we honestly believe they are wrong, we have to face the question of why they should be excused from obligations that others have to discharge, much as they would prefer not to.

Many feel that that these judgements fail to capture the moral complexity of issues about war and peace. Even those who are not pacifists may consider pacifism a noble position. In a perfect world, there would be no killing. The issue between pacifist and non-pacifist is how far one should be prepared to fall short of a moral ideal in an imperfect world. The pacifist position is an archetypal absolutist one, enforcing a rule, regardless of circumstances, and allowing no exceptions. It has a certain moral purity about it, and pacifists perhaps perform a valuable function in reminding us of the horrors of war.

It may then be too easy to say that conscientious objectors are simply mistaken, or are indulging private sensibilities. The view that killing is wrong has to go very deep in any moral understanding of the world. Anyone must accept that killing could only be justified in special circumstances, and they are usually where human lives are at stake, whatever we do. The conscientious objector is distinguished from the rest of us in refusing to participate in what is wrong, no matter what the consequences. How far this is an admirable pursuit of moral perfection, and how far sheer irresponsibility, is a fit subject of moral debate. It is not likely to be quickly resolved, and the issue is how the majority treat the minority who disagree. Moral divergence, and indeed the right to be mistaken, is the necessary result of freedom of choice. As we have seen, the imposition of morality can itself be an attack on the basis of morality. A conformist society, where people do as they are told, is not a society of morally responsible individuals.

Views of morality, which talk of moral truth, can be accused of leading to intolerance, and to the stifling of the individual conscience. Once morality is enforced simply because it is the view of a particular society, the situation becomes similar to relativist views of society. There is then no scope for disagreement about what is true, or for individuals to follow their own beliefs. Yet there have been prophets who have had the courage to say that a whole society is mistaken. We have only to think of the abolition of slavery, or the more recent abolition of apartheid, to see that there is sometimes a need for moral visionaries to stand out against a society. Treatment of conscientious objectors as simply mistaken does not take the importance of individual moral judgement seriously.

There is a delicate balance here because one does not want to fall into a subjectivism that says that what each person decides is right for that individual. Yet, at the same time, it is unrealistic, given human fallibility, to hope that any one person, or group, can have complete moral understanding. To say that conscientious objectors will not be forced to conform is to take a principled approach to moral disagreement. It is to accept that moral divisions themselves have to be reflected in the application of law. This is different from an easy acquiescence in diversity for the sake of diversity. It is to recognize the seriousness of the moral challenge presented by pacifism and the refusal to fight.

The question of how far one can opt out of the obligation to defend one's country is always going to be a vexed one. Indeed, for a long period in the early twentieth century, the United States would not allow avowed pacifists to become naturalized citizens. In 1929, for instance, citizenship was denied to a woman pacifist on precisely that ground, even though she was already disqualified from military service by sex and age. Now, as long as conscientious objection is linked to some form of religious belief, it is no longer a bar to citizenship. In Britain, as long as it could be proved that conscientious objection was the product of a long and settled belief, it was, in the days of conscription, a ground for refusing to serve in the armed forces.

Moral judgements, made out of a principle, should be tolerated in a free society, as far as possible, even though they are at variance with majority opinion. A failure to contribute to society, and to fulfil the obligations of citizenship, is one thing, but it is quite another to be compelled to do what one believes in a firm way to be wrong. At the same time there has to be a public policy on some matters. Those responsible for implementing it may sometimes find it so morally repugnant that they may even have to resign. Doctors and nurses expected to participate in abortions may find that this goes against deeply held beliefs, and have to choose between their post and their beliefs. Judges, when faced with enforcing laws they object to (say over capital punishment), can step down rather than do so. Up to a point, in a democratic society we should expect policy to be carried out even by those who disagree with it. There is, however, a difference between ordinary disagreement over the wisdom or effectiveness of a course of action, and a deeply held moral principle over the value of human life, which is allegedly being broken.

The point about citizenship and conscientious objection is that one cannot easily renounce one's citizenship, unlike resigning one's job. We are left having to decide whether we simply want a society enforcing its will, or one that takes morality so seriously that it has to accommodate moral disputes even when its survival is at stake. Toleration of other people's consciences about serious matters, even when most think they are mistaken, is in fact a recognition of the importance of morality as a basis for society. We dare not ride roughshod over other people's moral principles because, if we do, we imply that morality is less important than conformity. Yet that itself is a path to relativism. Moral matters can never be settled by majority vote, even if political action has to be. An important aspect of the objectivity of morality is that mistake and error are always possible. Respect for the views of those with whom we deeply disagree reminds us of that simple truth.

Notes

1   William Galston, *Liberal Pluralism*, Cambridge University Press, Cambridge, 2002, p. 72.
2   Ibid., p. 73.
3   Ibid.
4   Ibid., p. 75.
5   Robert George, *In Defense of Natural Law*, Oxford University Press, New York, 1999, p. 110.
6   Ibid., p. 111.
7   Hadley Arkes, *First Things: An Inquiry into the First Principles of Morals and Justice*, Princeton University Press, Princeton, NJ, 1986, p. 42.
8   Ibid., p. 31.

6

The public and
the private

Is a Political Pluralism Ethically Neutral?

Despite divergences in the moral principles we may wish to espouse, we have seen that morality must ultimately be concerned with what is good and bad for human beings. Serious moral disagreements must typically be about precisely this. We can sympathize with the pacifist insistence that taking human life is the ultimate evil, while recognizing that situations may be very complicated, and greater harm may ensue, and more lives may be lost, by refusing to do so. Morality is about what helps us all to do well, and in this sense a recognition of so-called natural law is merely a recognition of what helps and hinders our welfare because of our shared human nature. It involves, too, accepting the natural equality that obtains between all of us. Yet there is clearly still great scope here for honest disagreement.

This understanding of morality stresses our understanding of objective circumstances in the world. We can be mistaken about what helps humans. The universality of natural law is also relevant. One does not need to be an American or an African to see what causes harm, any more than it is of assistance to be Chinese or European. We can all see how the world works and how it impinges on human nature. For example, physical pain is no respecter of national boundaries. It is part of our human make-up to feel it, and one should need no great theory to understand that inflicting unnecessary pain is morally repugnant. In more complicated matters, there will be an element of judgement, governed by various preconceptions, and even world-views. Not everyone will see costs and benefits in the same way. In the end, though, such judgements are not arbitrary. Truth is at stake.

The stress on the objectivity of the factors relevant for moral decisions, and the expectation that they are universally available, must challenge many current conceptions of morality. The separation of facts and values has led to a view of morality as being rationally detached from circumstances in the world. Morality is just about people and their attitudes and choices. This has led in politics to the idea that all a democracy has to do is to take account of the differing views of its members, without adjudicating between them. All that matters is that people may have strong beliefs, and that they have to be reconciled if we are all to live together. Such an idea is encouraged by, and helps to encourage, a strong view of ethical pluralism. This does not just accept that people disagree, but holds that there is no way in principle of resolving differences over morality.

A politics espousing pluralism in this sense leaves ethical judgement to the various groups and individuals making up a society. It does not take up a position about what is good, and may even take a pride in an avowed neutrality. It assumes this somehow makes a more just society, although the idea of what is just is itself a central moral notion. The idea is that the state's function is only to be an umpire, intent on allowing people to live together as best they can. Law is then to be merely regulatory, so that citizens can live as they choose, without having any particular view of what makes a good society, or a good life, imposed on them. When views clash, there will have to be political negotiation and compromise. There is in this picture no place in public life for a substantive moral argument to decide who is right.

An example might be the demand of some Muslim women that they keep their face veiled in public. This may not be the custom of other groups, but in a democratic society it might appear wrong to insist that women appear unveiled if they do not wish to do so. There is no need to argue about whether women should behave in this way. Some may wish to, and their wishes should be respected. Yet what happens when the law demands a photograph of someone's face, for the purposes of identification, whether in a passport or on a driving licence? A woman may profoundly object to being seen unveiled. Yet she may wish to travel, or drive. At this point, political considerations may come into play, not least those of security. Allowing photographs of someone veiled, or alternatively no photograph at all, may create unacceptable security risks of various kinds. The majority may decide that political interests demand that the woman's beliefs not be respected.

At no point in all this argument would the basic issue of the veiling of women be addressed. Even if, in some people's eyes, it is a symbol of an immoral subjugation of women, the issue is left on one side. Women's wishes are merely accepted as a fact, without any further ethical question being raised. The only problem is the political one about what can and what cannot be tolerated in the interests of living together. Yet even this apparently neutral position, refusing to take sides about the worth of certain practices, carries with it an assumption of what a good society is. It is a democratic one, where majorities decide, but where differences between people are acknowledged, and, as far as possible, maintained. Diversity becomes valued for its own sake, and toleration becomes the major virtue.

Pluralism, however, may begin by noting the fact of difference, but it quickly comes to accept that it is actually desirable. It follows that no one particular conception of the good should be given precedence. An ethically neutral position soon becomes an ethically charged one. The aim is a pluralist, preferably multicultural, society, where freedom in moral matters is to be regarded as the highest good, subject only to the constraints of our being able to live together. Respect for difference becomes an ethical principle, instead of being regarded as an obstacle on the way to moral agreement. Anyone who wishes to impose their view on others, or even dares to suggest that their view is the right one, must be seen as challenging the very fabric of society. A shared morality, instead of being the glue that holds a community together, comes to be seen as a challenge to its very existence.

Ethical neutrality is somehow combined with a substantive notion of what kind of society we ought to have. Tolerance is preached, and intolerance to those who would prefer a different kind of society is actually practised. Any idea that society should be rooted in a single conception of what is good is opposed in the name of what is itself a single conception of the good. Thus the 'neutral' and 'liberal' society will be avowedly secular. It will be opposed to any Islamic society which tries to base itself on the Koran alone. It will be opposed to the idea of an established Church in Western countries which sets particular standards, in however vague and benevolent a manner.

This latter point gives the clue to some of the historical roots of liberalism, particularly of the American variety. It comes out of the American distrust of any hierarchy of Anglican bishops, and the determination to allow freedom of religion in the United States. Yet there has always been an ambiguity even here. The same American coins which today proclaim 'Liberty' also say that 'In God We Trust'. They also claim that the United States constitutes *e pluribus unum*, one out of many. The whole conundrum becomes explicit in these messages. Liberty demands that people have the freedom to live as they wish, yet the reference to God suggests that the state has a religious basis, of a particular kind. The God invoked may be the God of Muslims and Jews, as well as of Catholics and Presbyterians. He is certainly not the God of atheists, and probably not of Buddhists and others. Yet we return to the problem of whether a society can exist as a society without some shared conception of what is good. Any society, or community, has to be more than a conglomeration of different people, happening to be together in one place at one time. Any society, by definition, has to be in some sense 'one' as well as being composed of 'many'. A crowd of people hurrying across an airport concourse on their way to and from different continents, some only in that country to change planes, are all in one place together. They spring from diverse traditions and customs, and speak many different languages. Yet they cannot be a 'society'.

The 'Veil of Ignorance'

What more is needed, at least so that people can live together? As we saw in the Introduction, the liberal conception of a society has found eloquent expression in the work of the American political philosopher John Rawls. His 'veil of ignorance' would shield the parties to an imaginary social contract from specific beliefs about what is good and bad. Any agreement would therefore not be undertaken merely to further particular interests. They would not know, in trying to organize a society, which beliefs they would actually have in it. As Rawls says, 'Putting people's comprehensive doctrines behind a veil of ignorance enables us to find a political conception of justice that can be the focus of an overlapping consensus, and thereby serve as a public basis of justification in a society marked by the fact of reasonable pluralism.'[1] The idea is that all substantive beliefs about what is good and bad, stemming from particular traditions, would be put on one side when we decide what a fair and just society would look like. We should not favour one because we considered it right, because, behind the veil of ignorance, we would not know whether that would be the belief that we would actually hold in a real society. Thus we would have to favour impartiality between beliefs. Rawls says that we have to assume the society is 'pluralistic', although even then there have to be some limits about the beliefs to be tolerated. They would not be ruled out because they were false, or because we disagreed with them. The ground could only be political, in the sense that they were illiberal, and made the establishment of a 'just' society impossible. What is needed is political consensus, not agreement on truth.

This way of looking at things means that the kind of reasoning allowed in the public sphere is going to be markedly different from what individuals might use privately. There is a radical split between the 'public' and the 'private', between what is allowed in a social setting and what individuals can privately believe. The idea is that, given the fact of different beliefs and traditions coexisting in one society, they cannot live together with the imposition of some shared vision. There can only be agreement about the procedures and laws necessary for living together, and settling disputes about how we can do this. Any arguments in the public sphere must then be acceptable to those who disagree on very fundamental matters. The aim is to allow maximum freedom to each other to live by one's beliefs, without interfering in what others do.

The ensuing break between public and private can hardly be clear-cut, but it forms a fundamental part of many conceptions of political liberalism. It is not an unfamiliar idea to those who have to combine public roles with strong personal beliefs. An example might be judges or magistrates who have to enforce the law of the land, as it is, and not as they would like it to be. Members of licensing authorities might have personal objections to the ready availability of alcohol, but that does not mean they should refuse an application for a licence to sell it if the application is in order from a legal point of view. There would have to be identifiable public grounds for doing so, such as a threat to public order. The enforcement of public law can never be allowed to be a parade of private conviction. Private beliefs and public roles are separate, and the picture of the veil of ignorance invokes this fact. The structures of society, and the procedures by which we are governed, cannot become the plaything of those with personal causes to fight for.

Rawls says at one point: 'Accounts of human nature we put aside, and rely on a political conception of persons as citizens instead.'[2] The problem is that any conception of human nature will be freighted with views of what is good. Indeed, that is the whole point of ideas of natural law. Rawls thinks that we have to concentrate on the relationship of people in a political arena, where pluralism of belief cannot be eradicated. The moral conception of justice has to be placed on one side, in favour of a political one. We cannot be concerned in this context with the nature of the world, or of human nature in it, since our focus must be on obtaining consensus. We do not collectively decide what is good, but negotiate how best to live with one another, and tolerate one another's behaviour.

This can seem a tempting position when we are confronted with a diversity of opinion on important questions, and no clear way of resolving the disputes. We can conclude that we should not resolve them but instead find ways of living with them. Yet the tension remains. We still have to decide whether we are willing to live in the kind of society that does, or does not, allow abortion. There appears to be no way any society can avoid the choice. Leaving it to individual choice may be the liberal option, but it will not satisfy those who want to outlaw abortion completely. Restricting, or even forbidding, abortion will not, on the other hand, meet the demands of those for whom a freedom to choose would be of major importance. There is, in the last resort, no neutral position here. Some group is going to be offended. A political negotiation, which produces a compromise, might be possible. The circumstances in which abortion is to be allowed might be defined in law. That is unlikely to appease those who see abortion as murder, any more than it satisfies those who see any restriction as an invasion of individual liberty. Two moral principles collide, and a political consensus is likely to be difficult. Each side wants victory. That was the precisely the kind of situation Rawls used the veil of ignorance to circumvent.

Liberalism may pursue neutrality over moral issues, and attempt to turn morality, at least at the public level, into political negotiation. Yet its preference for diversity and tolerance itself picks out certain features of society and gives them moral weight. It is itself sometimes ambivalent about how far it is searching for compromise, and how far it demands certain solutions. A liberal might search for common ground, or at least compromise, between the various entrenched positions over abortion. In that case an absolute right, whether to 'life' or to 'choice', would be ruled out. Those behind a veil of ignorance could consider this a just solution. On the other hand, some liberals might see individual freedom as of paramount importance, and support a right for a woman to choose. Either way, it is clear that those upholding a 'right to life' are being challenged.

The emphasis on the importance of procedure, not content, and the delight in diversity are linked with a vision of democracy at work. For the liberal, social unity lies in the acknowledgement of settled procedures and laws for the regulation of society that do not interfere with particular ways of life. The stress on individual freedom carries with it an assumption that citizens must be left to use that freedom as they wish, even in the most important areas of morality. The state should not interfere, prejudge issues or favour any particular outcomes. Yet there is a paradox in all this. Something still has to bind a state together, if it is only respect for its laws, and that respect is itself only secure if it has proper moral basis.

The Moral Basis of Agreement

Changing the subject from morality to politics, from moral argument to a search for political compromise, requires an explicit willingness to follow particular procedures, and abide by their results. Moral teaching may be replaced in schools by civics classes about the duties of a citizen. Yet reference to 'duties' merely shows that morality cannot be written out of the script that easily. Many theories of society, such as Rawls's theory of justice, rely on the idea of a contract between individuals. They all need the parties to the contract to feel under some obligation to continue keeping the contract, even when it is inconvenient to do so. In the abstract, behind a veil of ignorance, we might condemn those who take advantage of other people's integrity while seeking personal advantage. In the real world, however, we know that all too often people will break the rules if they think they can get away with doing so. Again, the issue is integrity. Without a moral basis, recognized by participants, any system of rules or law will only be effective in so far as it can be enforced.

Any 'procedural' notion of a just society, which places stress on systems, and not integrity, on 'public' laws, and not 'private' morality, pays attention to what can be publicly agreed, without enforcing any one view of morality. Yet it is an illusion to think that any of this can be sustained without a moral outlook. We have to have some assurance that people enter political negotiations in good faith, and intend to abide by the outcome. Honesty and integrity are the presupposition of agreements, not their product. A contract is no contract at all if it is kept only when it is convenient to do so.

The old motto of the City of London was that 'my word is my bond'. Once financial traders take advantage of the presumption of honesty, and of other people's integrity, to cheat, deceive and manipulate, the whole apparatus of financial dealing is put in danger. Corporations that misrepresent their profits, and accountants who cut corners, may do well in the short term, but, if they are found out, confidence in the whole system can ebb away. It is in everyone's interest to be honest. Cheating may push up share prices this year, but it is not a sustainable long-term policy. It is, therefore, rational, it may appear, both to agree not to cheat and to keep to the agreement. The trouble is that although it may be a matter of enlightened self-interest to do so normally, there may be times where dishonesty might succeed, because it may never be found out. Some will still be tempted to run that risk, even after they have made an agreement not to. Yet from the moral point of view, it must be regarded as deeply wrong, whatever one's estimate of the likely consequences. Too many taking that kind of risk will soon undermine the whole financial system. What happens on the public stage can only be effective given a background of private honesty and integrity.

Any view that sees obligations as merely created by agreements must still accept that any agreement has to have force even when it is inconvenient to keep it. In other words, parties to the agreement have to have a moral outlook already formed. It must give them a sense of what is right, and a willingness to abide by it, even when it is in their own interests not to do so. The problem is that a liberal picture of society is one where morality is a private matter, and public reason may not appeal to private, individual moral beliefs. Yet at the same time it depends on tacit, or actual, agreements and promises to live by certain public procedures, and to follow them in good faith. It is all very individualist, in that it starts from a number of individuals, regarding them as a collection of atoms. They are unrelated to each other in any way, yet are liable to collide. There is no wider vision of society, or of morality, as its basis. The 'public square' may be one where individuals congregate, and establish ways of living together, but their own private attitudes remain, and are not moulded or harnessed to the common good. The stability of the whole may depend on the character and principles of the participants, but liberal doctrine wants to remain neutral as to what those should be. As we shall see later, this is a deep problem for liberalism.

Any society needs a morality, and cannot last without some shared assumptions. Even liberalism itself, as we have seen, has to assume integrity and honesty in abiding by publicly agreed rules. The most liberal of societies will find that it may need citizenship classes in its schools, which are far from neutral in moral outlook. They will prescribe a particular way of living together, as encapsulated in the legal framework of that society. They will also inevitably have to teach that it is right to abide by its rules and procedures, and that those who do not are blameworthy. Trust between citizens is a precondition of social life. That, together with honesty, cannot be negotiable if a society is to function at all.

It is easy to concentrate on particular moral disagreements within a society, and to forget that they can only take place against a background of wider agreement on what is necessary to keep a society together. Shared moral values have to provide a glue. The issue is how much disagreement can occur before a society begins to splinter. This not just an intellectual problem. Modern societies are complex, and subject to diverse influences. Yet the greater the diversity, the more difficult it is to form any unity, and to forge bonds of mutual trust. Some try to resist these pressures by demanding strict controls on immigration into their country. Yet this evades the basic issue, about the understandings necessary for us to live together. Blaming some particular group for the disruption of past agreements evades the question of the moral foundation of those agreements.

Trust

Trust between citizens is an absolute precondition for any cooperation. Yet such trust cannot be taken for granted, and it is consistent with a liberal outlook that we cannot assume honesty. When public procedures are sharply distinguished from private, and individual, moral stances, public attention will be concentrated on those procedures. Honesty has to be enforced, and checked, by public means, if it is thought publicly desirable. It cannot be left to personal character. People can thus only be trusted if their performance is tested in publicly verifiable ways. To take the market as a model, transactions there have to be checkable, since we must not take traders' honesty at face value. Yet this ignores the basic fact that any transaction, from a social contract to buying vegetables, has to invoke a shared moral understanding if it is to succeed. All negotiations need a background of trust. If money is to change hands, we must assume it is genuine, not forged. We have to trust a trader to give us the amount and quality of vegetables we asked for, rather than using faulty scales, or hiding the rotten ones at the bottom of a bag. Things can on occasion go wrong, but if people were always dishonest, no one would buy or sell anything. Social life would break down.

What happens in a market for farm produce is replicated in financial markets. Trust between individuals and confidence in the system are an absolute precondition for business. When money loses its value, it cannot be an instrument of exchange. If corruption becomes rife, capitalism can no longer function. All markets have to convey information about what people want to buy, and what they want to sell. This delicate price mechanism can be perverted if bribes, and other extraneous influences, have an influence. Prices may no longer accurately reflect the interests of buyers or sellers, and the system will begin to break down. Once people lose confidence, other means, such as barter, will be found to facilitate the exchange of goods. Economic freedom only makes sense if it is given a moral foundation, of which reliability, honesty and personal integrity are an indispensable part. Financial institutions may attempt to meet the threat posed by personal dishonesty by introducing regulators and 'watchdogs'. Yet the more necessary these are seen to be, the more the system must be in some state of disrepair. Without abuses, public checking would not be necessary.

Total economic freedom might seem to go with a total moral freedom to choose what way of life we like. Is not freedom indivisible? It is a paradox, though, that radical freedom over morality actually undermines economic freedom. It cannot be left to us as individuals to decide how honest we shall be. Yet liberals typically favour total moral freedom, but are more suspicious of economic freedom. They are concerned with what they view as social justice, so that the poor and the sick are given help, even if they cannot pay for it themselves. Social justice, however, is itself a moral notion. The reverse problem holds with those who may be more conservative socially. They typically favour a strong version of economic freedom, which may favour the creation of wealth, but ignores those who are disadvantaged. The strong will prosper, while others do less well, and are even exploited. Yet these 'conservatives' will be likely to favour a strong moral code in society, which favours a traditional morality, and advocates honesty and trustworthiness. They will resist any suggestion that individuals should decide for themselves not only whether to be moral, but also what that is to mean for them. If morality really is the glue holding a society together, both liberals and conservatives are only concentrating on part of the story. Untrustworthiness can undermine a society, and so can excessive inequality, and disparity of treatment, particularly if it leads to significant suffering. At the extreme, it can provoke revolution. Any society has to be concerned about the well-being of all its citizens. It may not consider total economic equality either possible or desirable, but that does not mean that it can ignore sections of a population whose plight is desperate, particularly if it is through no fault of their own.

The ebbing away of mutual trust remains a major threat. Even when institutions, and regulatory bodies, are formed to enforce fair dealing, they themselves still depend on trust. For example, regulatory bodies, in education and other fields in Britain, often rely on written 'evidence' that something has been done. An attitude of mind can develop that if an event has not been recorded, it has not happened. Forms are provided for boxes to be ticked to ensure that correct procedures have been followed by the police. Minutes of meetings show what was discussed. Teachers have to provide detailed written plans for what is taught. Public evidence is required to reassure us that what should have happened has happened. This is fallacious, as sloppy paperwork does not necessarily imply sloppy teaching, or a failure to follow proper legal procedure. Inspirational teachers, or conscientious police, may still be bad administrators.

'Fair Play'

The problem is that if a stress is put on the necessity for public evidence, it is then taken at face value. Yet if we really take seriously the breakdown of trust that all these procedures exemplify, there seems little reason to trust those providing the documents. Agencies are set up to monitor those who in previous generations were considered to have high professional standards. Once the suspicion of deceit enters the system, there can be no stopping its corrosive power. Corrupt police are not going to be unduly concerned about forging forms, or pretending correct procedures have been followed. Minutes can be concocted for imaginary meetings, and superb teaching notes can be drawn up portraying lessons that never took place. Dishonesty is never going to be thwarted by regulation. A response may then be to increase the intrusiveness of regulation, but an atmosphere of distrust can then raise questions about the competence and integrity of the regulators. It is not unknown in British universities for a team of inspectors to be monitored during their inspection by another team checking them.

The weight of regulation can in the end be increased to the point where it destroys what is being regulated. Without trust, however, there is never a point at which doubt can be removed. There can be no ultimate assurance that any process of checking can be relied on any more than can those who are investigated. Suspicion feeds on itself, and no public process can escape it. Regulation demands the very probity of character that it refuses to acknowledge in those being regulated. Much of such regulation is carried out in the name of so-called democratic 'accountability'. The idea is that in a democracy those with a public role should be accountable to their fellow citizens, particularly if public money is being spent. Yet it is one thing to have moral responsibilities to one's fellow citizens. It is another to have to prove to them continually that one is fulfilling them. The emphasis will then inevitably move from the responsibility to the mode of proof, from what I am doing to what I can make myself appear to other people to be doing. Presentation, and marketing, can overwhelm reality.

Democracy does not depend on the demonstration of trustworthiness. Trust has to be the bedrock, and starting point, for democracy. If elected representatives, and officials, cannot be trusted to be concerned with our interests, faith in democracy will wither. When citizens come to believe that they are merely being manipulated by clever presentation of policy, they will become cynical. Once it is thought that politicians are only concerned with their own advantage, loyalty to a form of government will not run deep. Similarly, citizens have to be able to trust the democratic process. Elections have to be fair, and not rigged. We have to trust each other to abide by the rules. An old adage in Northern Ireland elections was said (perhaps unfairly) to be 'Vote early, vote often'. Impersonation was alleged to be rife. Yet this kind of activity must very quickly bring the whole of democratic politics into disrepute.

Agreements can only be made, and then respected, in a context in which we can rely on each other, and on those who represent us. Once it is accepted that the responsibilities of those who are properly called public servants, whether in government or civil service, are subordinated to other interests, cynicism will grow into disaffection. Once it is accepted that our fellow citizens are not going to abide by decisions they do not like, when they are in a minority, again democracy will dissolve into chaos. We have to trust that the opposing parties will each be loyal to the constitution, and not take to the streets when it suits them. Democracy does not create the conditions for trust. It depends on the prior existence of mutual respect between citizens. They have to trust each other, and they must themselves be willing to be trustworthy, even when it goes against their own immediate interests.

All this has implications for a 'liberal' belief in individual freedom. Any democracy should safeguard that, but autonomy can never be absolute if we are to be linked together in mutual relationships, and are to cooperate in a society. A culture of public accountability is the inevitable result of encouraging a freedom that can be used to disregard other people's interests. 'Performance indicators' then become necessary to prove that people are fulfilling their particular responsibilities. The emphasis in many jobs becomes one of how to look good in statistics. Yet all efforts to make others accountable will fail if no one personally feels any prior moral responsibility, or loyalty to any principles. Nothing can replace the judgement that we each must be concerned with the interests of others, and that others can rely on us to fulfil whatever our own responsibilities are. Autonomy must have its limits. No society can be stable once its members are taught that there is no objective standard of morality, but that it is a private decision for each of them whether or not to pursue their own advantage at the expense of others. No one can be compelled to be good in a free society, but that is different from maintaining an official, and public, neutrality about the worth of honesty and reliability. Moral education is essential in any society, and cannot be so neutral that it can pretend that character is absolutely a matter of personal choice. It does matter for the sake of a society what kind of person we become. 'Self-expression', 'self-development', 'realizing oneself' and other terms, which may stress the centrality of the self, can ignore the way in which other people depend on us, and we depend on others. Some character traits, related to personal integrity, are not optional if society is not to be put at risk.

Those who wish to live in a tolerant society can easily overestimate the amount of freedom which can be encouraged in moral matters. The temptation in the face of radical disagreement is to search for the maximum amount of freedom for people to live according to their own beliefs. It may seem that a free society, which rejoices in diversity, can be neutral, if not indifferent, to moral concerns. The ideal is made to appear to be the neutral referee ensuring fair play without supporting either side. Yet even if the role of society is seen as merely the neutral enforcement of rules to enable us to live together, that requires a large background of training and education for its citizens. We all have to understand the implicit, and explicit, rules. The players of a game, such as football, have to be taught the letter and spirit of the rules of a game. They cannot even play it without many shared assumptions about what is and what is not acceptable. The neutrality of the referee comes in not favouring one side. It is not a matter of being indifferent about what the rules of the game are. In the same way, society should be neutral (or just) in the way it enforces its rules. 'Fair play' is important. It cannot stop caring about which rules are to be enforced.

The old phrase alluding to 'honour among thieves' shows that any social group depends for its existence on mutual trust. A network of trust and mutual confidence must be the foundation of any collective activity. A society fostering an extreme individualism must be a contradiction in terms. It cannot go on being constituted by separate individuals, each making decisions as to what is to count as right and wrong, without any reference to others. We all have to be willing to adhere to the rules of a society, whether we are seen to do so or not. Our private commitments must match our public professions. A trust that our fellow citizens will be doing that has to be matched by a principled willingness to do the same oneself, even at a cost. That is what loyalty means.

There is always a moral problem as to how far any loyalty should be stretched. Some institutions may betray it. Some countries do not deserve the loyalty of their citizens. Yet the existence of dilemmas, such as the duty of a German under the Nazis, only illustrates the point that each of us is set in a wider social context in which demands for our loyalty are made. The dilemmas arise when there are countervailing moral claims. They are only dilemmas, though, because the claim of loyalty is there. Every society has to demand it, even if there may be occasions when it should be withheld. No human institution can survive without a loyalty that asks me to sacrifice my interests at times for the benefit of others. Private morality is not separate from the existence of public and social interaction. It is the precondition for it. How we decide to live affects those around us. None of us can forget that we all live in groups, and in social settings, and have obligations that go far beyond our own particular wishes.

Notes

1   John Rawls, *The Law of Peoples*, Harvard University Press, Cambridge, MA, 1999, p. 32.
2   Ibid., p. 172.

7

Groups and individuals

Which Differences Matter Morally?

As human beings, we all belong to groups of one kind and another. This raises the question as to how far the mere fact of such membership is itself of moral significance. Morality seems to call for an identification with institutions, and with groups of other people. We incur obligations to them. The idea that I alone matter is pernicious, as is the notion that my concerns, however arbitrary, should absorb my attention. Some associations are purely voluntary. I can choose whether or not to join a golf club, and abide by its rules. Members sign up because they want to play golf with others, and resign when they lose interest, when they get old or when their spouses complain that they are never home. Not all groupings are like this, and many seem much more intimately bound up with the kind of people we are. My identity often appears linked with questions of which group I belong to. Nationality, sex, race, class and education are only some of the more obvious factors that may appear to define us. They may certainly be central in how we experience the world.

Being English may be very important to some, even if they have long lived in another part of the world. That is not the issue here. Should someone be treated differently because they are English? Is it a morally relevant category? Perhaps their likes and dislikes have been influenced by their upbringing, and it may be morally important to take these into account. Yet we do this on the principle of being attentive to other people's individual needs, not because we put them into a general category. It is unwise to assume that all English people will prefer tea to coffee.

This may seem obvious, but there are powerful currents flowing, which result in the idea that membership of a group, defined in various ways, is morally significant. The issue is then not about tastes, but about the question of whether those from particular backgrounds, who are members of particular groups, have obtained unfair advantages or suffered unjust disadvantages. The individual is seen as part of a group. What is true of the group is then thought to apply to all its members, and to be morally decisive.

This view has many practical effects. For example, those seeking admission to universities come from many different backgrounds. Some have had great advantages, and others have not. Society has placed obstacles in the way of some, and made the way easier for others. Any decision may well have to take this into account. A poorly prepared student from an indifferent school may have greater potential than someone else who has reached the same standard after receiving an education in a fine school. Yet the difficulty comes when we stop looking at individuals and their personal background. Instead, we allow the background to define the individual, and treat individuals as members of a class to be treated in a particular way. Then, for example, all that matters is whether someone, in an English context, has been to a state school or an independent fee-paying one. Someone from the former is then preferred over someone from the latter, on the grounds that most pupils in independent schools are likely to have a more privileged background than those from state schools. Yet if individual circumstances are ignored, this may mean that the son or daughter of a millionaire at a state school in a fashionable area is admitted to university, rather than someone who has been awarded a scholarship from a poor background to a fee-paying school.

Membership of a group, however understood, should not be enough to justify someone being treated in a particular way. What matters is the need of individuals, not the fact that they belong to a certain class. Class distinction, racism and other forms of unjust discrimination all make the mistake of defining an individual by their group. People are treated differently not because of who they individually are, but because of some way in which they are classified. This is just as pernicious when they are going to be treated better than other people as when they are going to be treated worse. There have, though, been many examples of injustice to groups in recent history. Often the groups have been defined racially. Indigenous inhabitants of countries which have received white settlers may feel their ancestors were badly treated. Maoris in New Zealand, Aborigines in Australia and American Indians are only part of a long list. Many in Ireland still suffer a sense of grievance over the way their predecessors suffered in the potato famine.

The question then arises as to whether apologies should be made and reparations given by the current representatives of whatever group is held responsible. Collective need and collective guilt are both alleged. There is clearly room for much argument about historical facts, but the root of the matter is that, whatever injustice there has been in the past, it is unclear whether need, and guilt, can be transmitted collectively, so that I am responsible for what my ancestors did, while you are owed something because of what your ancestors suffered. This only becomes applicable if membership of a group is morally relevant, in a way that individual responsibility is not. Yet, to take a different kind of example, one of the objections to massive acts of terrorism is that they are aimed at people as representatives of a group, and not as individuals. As one writer puts it, 'terrorism is itself one of the most immoral forms of collective punishment against innocent people based on their religion, nationality or location'.[1] Certainly a possible (and equally immoral) response to terrorism is to punish groups indiscriminately. This was certainly a technique favoured by Hitler and the Nazis in reprisals, after, say, an attack by resistance fighters.

One possible argument is that, because a group suffered great injustice in the past, there have been created structural divides in society that have not been overcome. Thus membership of a particular group still carries with it particular penalties. It is the present reason for present unfairness. Amy Gutmann has put the problem well in connection with race in the United States. She says: 'The government can't be color blind because society isn't – people and institutions treat citizens differently according to whether they are black or white, yellow or brown, and this fact raises questions of fairness.'[2] Much of this depends on the empirical question about whether, in a given society, racial consciousness does underwrite difference of treatment. No doubt racial differences do create the most obviously identifiable groups. In many societies this can form the basis for different treatment, even withholding the franchise. What is the moral response? Amy Gutmann makes the point that in any society political divisions will divide by groups, since, she says, 'effective democratic politics is by its very nature group politics'.[3] Interest groups, bound together by a common interest, are the very stuff of democracy, but the crucial question is how far the groups are picked out by morally relevant features. The mere fact that they all have the same desires may not make them especially deserving. Groups that are formed to fight for an issue (perhaps to stop a road being built) have no greater substance than is given by the agreement to cooperate.

Which differences create a moral case for difference in treatment and which do not? Some groups may define themselves into existence, while others are genuine victims. Yet should the moral basis for a difference in treatment rest on my identification with a group, class or race, rather than something about me personally? The question is whether it can be morally relevant that I am white or black, or of this country or that. Personal needs are then defined by those of my group. Amy Gutmann even defends the fact that we ought to be conscious of a person's colour. In the face of 'colour blindness', which many would regard as an essential part of morality, she argues as follows:

> Color consciousness faces up to the fact that Americans today are still identified by their color, and treated in distinct, often morally indefensible ways, by virtue of it. Not to be color conscious is not to face up to this fact. The color of Americans significantly affects their life chances and experiences, not for essentialist reasons, but for no less significant historical and social reasons, which no single individual is sufficiently powerful to change.[4]

Past wrongs can only righted, it seems, by deliberate policy from institutions and government that past wrongs can be righted. Similar arguments are mounted in many societies, but there is in the United States a particularly powerful sense of past racial injustice. Because skin colour has been the occasion of historical wrongs, it is taken to be of moral significance now. Membership of particular racial groups is thus still seen as morally relevant.

Discrimination and Multiculturalism

'Discrimination' has become a label for immoral differentiation, but, in one sense, discriminating between people is the basis of morality. How do I know whom to help if I cannot discriminate between those who are in need and those who are not? The point is not that people are treated differently, but whether the basis for any distinction is itself moral. Unless I am willing to reject the whole structure of moral argument, I have to recognize the relevance of other people's needs, just as I want them to recognize mine. Exceptions in my own favour are rarely justifiable, and the same argument can be applied at the level of groups. Needs and interests cannot be recognized simply on the grounds that they arise from *my* group. There has to be a special reason that makes them distinctive.

Racial distinctions, and, in particular, those that are attached to physical characteristics, would not seem to be very promising candidates for moral relevance. Why should the shape of a nose, or the colour of skin, be of any more relevance than the colour of one's hair? Skin colour could matter in very circumscribed areas, as when someone with a very fair skin might be more vulnerable to sunburn, and even skin cancer. This could be morally relevant if one had to choose between a fair and dark skinned person to spend time in the sun. This, though, is an issue about skin. 'Race', as picked out by physical characteristics, is not linked to anything else that could be of moral importance.

Some may try to make a link between race and culture, and suggest that one could predict someone's behaviour, or beliefs, on the basis of racial origin. This is hardly likely to be true in an age when there is so much contact between cultures, and so much intermingling of races. There is a tendency to link 'multiculturalism', and the encouragement of cultural diversity in one society, with an opposition to racism. Yet there is bound to be tension between opposition to racial discrimination and associating race and culture. The more that the two are linked, the more race itself will seem to be an important concept for defining identity. Principled opposition to a particular practice in a culture (such as the treatment of women) could then be made to look like racial prejudice. The only sure basis for attacking racial discrimination is to deny that the concept of race can have any morally relevant content.

'Multiculturalism' has to be a red herring in the quest for racial justice. Culture and race will only be contingently related, and in any case individuals can be subject to influences from many cultures. Amy Gutmann defines 'multiculturalism' in terms of individual choices. She claims: 'A society is openly multi-cultural to the extent that all individuals – depending on their appreciations and talents – have effective access to many cultural possibilities, no single one of which defines any person's identity, and all of which are subject to change by the creative efforts of individuals.'[5] This resonates with the American experience, and could even be said to be a feature of American culture. Its prime emphasis is on the individual, envisaged as coming with fully formed tastes and talents. On this view, culture does not create identity. We just choose which bits we want, in the way we might choose whether to go to a Chinese or a Greek restaurant.

A more controversial definition of multiculturalism might envisage separate cultures, each playing a positive role in forming the identity of its members. This can quickly turn into relativism, which regards any claim to superiority by one culture as cultural imperialism. When culture is linked to race, this becomes pictured as the attempt by one race to dominate another. Moral judgement in such circumstances becomes a species of racism. This is a nonsensical position, since if morality is subordinated to culture in this way, there is nowhere left to stand to be able to condemn racism itself. The criticism of attitudes to race, just as much as their assertion, becomes an expression of a particular culture.

'Culture' is a dangerous concept to link with moral views. Once the origins of such views are linked to a particular social or historical context they lose their ability to claim any universal application. They can be made to appear the prejudices of one group. Cultures are seen as wholes, setting their own standards, and unable to be judged rationally against a wider context. Rational argument will be replaced by domination and submission. 'Truth' will be ignored, or seen as an imperialist notion, something that can give rhetorical justification to a group's collective imposition of will. When that happens, proponents of so-called affirmative action programmes, tailored to further the interests of a group, could be seen as merely fighting a political battle on behalf of some group. Similarly, critics of such pro-grammes could be seen not as making any moral point, but as safeguarding the entrenched interests of the group to which they themselves belong. What should be a rational discussion about fairness and justice becomes transmuted into a raw power struggle. Morality becomes politics.

Politics, and the need for compromise and agreement, will have its place. There can be good political reasons for concentrating on the perceived interests of one group in order to redress past wrongs. An ongoing sense of injustice and bitterness can poison a whole society if no attempt is made to deal with it. Such action can be aimed at identifiable groups, rather than individuals, because such groups see themselves as victims. It may be important not just to replace unjust with just practices, but to do so in a very explicit way. Some would argue that favouring one group, even at the expense of others, could be seen as a way of healing long-lasting sores in a society. It should, though, be a short-term political gesture, signifying a change in the structure of that society.

The politics of this may vary from society to society, but the point is that it is politics, not morality. It is a policy designed to deal with a sense of injustice. It is not itself dealing justice, and carries risks. Once morality is put on one side, and the issue is the redressing of grievances, both real and imagined, everything can become a political struggle between factions and groups. A society depending on the shifting agreements of interest groups is insecurely based. A principled stand for justice for all is necessary in the longer term, so that morality, and not just politics, must be seen to matter.

groups and individuals

Some will see righting past injustices, on a group basis, as itself an expression of morality. The problem is that morality must begin with the individual, and be concerned with the individual. Ignoring an individual's interests, and seeing a person only as a type, or as a representative of a group, is the antithesis of this. Our revulsion at racism is an indication of this. A major moral objection to utilitarianism is the way in which it is willing to sacrifice the interests of individuals for the good of the whole. Even in that case, however, everyone counts as one in the initial calculation. Individuals and their interests are initially treated as of equal importance, even if, in the end, they are overridden. Utilitarianism works best as a route map for legislators, who by definition are establishing guidelines for society, and should not be concerned with individual circumstances. It is a question of deciding which laws promote the common good, not which help particular individuals. Laws cannot make exceptions, or have favourites. Justice demands that the law is administered without fear or favour.

When the law is applied, different considerations must come into play. The question of individual desert and responsibility must be considered. Utilitarianism is often tempted to run together the two issues. It does not only look at the wider social effects of its policies. It seems prepared to treat individuals as instruments in a wider social policy. While pursuing justice for all, it is prepared to commit great injustice in particular cases. Yet always the old conundrum must resurface. Does the end justify the means? Are we entitled to use repugnant and unfair methods even to achieve a highly desirable end?

The question becomes particularly acute in political contexts. When faced with the demands of interest groups, formed to exert democratic pressure, the temptation will be to search for political compromises with groups, rather than individuals. Any morality which ignores the realities of politics may appear naive, but, on the other hand, merely balancing interest groups against each other, on the basis of their power and influence, is not going to help the long-term stability of any society. Politics without morality, or, worse, a morality subordinated to the demands of the politics of the moment, must degenerate into shifting allegiances and uncertain outcomes. Balances of power, within societies and between societies, can change. Moral principles should not.

Treating individuals as representatives of a group is typical of a political approach. They are seen in terms of their wider place in society. Politicians may feel that membership of a race is significant, given prevailing social conditions, even if their aim is to discriminate in favour and not against a particular group. Yet whatever the social prejudices of the society, race should be strictly irrelevant from a moral point of view. Making it important is irrational, since there is no foundation in any doctrine of human nature to make arbitrary racial distinctions of any significance. Modern genetics has demonstrated there is as great variability of genes within so-called 'races' as between them. There is a biological foundation for talking of human nature, because all humans can inter-breed, and their genes form a common pool. There is none, though, for making meaningful subdivisions of humanity. The stress in neo-Darwinism has been on the selection of individuals, rather than groups. It may well be that culture, including morality, can have a beneficial, or harmful, effect on the flourishing of a society. In the end, however, the transmission of genes from one generation to the next is a matter for individuals, and any influence from a group has to be secondary, and mediated through the individual. Individuals, not groups or races, have offspring.

Racial distinctions have often been founded as much on differences of language, or religion, as on obvious physical characteristics. The distinctions which seem to matter are often the result of historical accident, geographical separation or political tensions within societies. There is no common thread running through apparent racial divides. The blond hair of the Saxon and the black hair of the Celt were once badges of difference in England, when Anglo-Saxons engulfed what had been a Celtic land. Now a millennium and a half later, the differences may still reappear, but they carry no message at all. Even if there are objective differences, the ones which appear salient seem a matter of historic contingency. Racial distinctions are a reflection of the society we live in, not of any underlying biology.

Taking some accidental feature, using it to identify a group and then treating someone as wholly defined by membership of that group is pernicious. It devalues our common humanity, in favour of some characteristic, real or imagined, that is used as a basis for difference of treatment. This approach simultaneously devalues the humanity we all share, and fails to take individuals seriously. Yet however much we may deplore racial prejudice, it has been an undoubted fact. It may seem unsurprising that honourable people should want to redress the wrongs of the past. When race has been such a potent symbol, can we pretend it has no significance? Even if we grant that there is little basis for discriminating on grounds of race alone, there may seem a case for tackling the socially constructed divisions within societies, rather than wishing they had not existed, and assuming they do not. In other words, affirmative action programmes to further the interests of a group, perhaps defined racially, could appear attractive. If in the past a group has been victimized, it might seem attractive to put things right, by giving the current representatives of that group greater opportunities. This issue goes to the heart of the issues we have been discussing as to whether people should be treated as individuals, or as stereotypical representatives of a group.

Recompense and reparation might appear just when groups have in the past been victims of appalling injustice. Yet the individuals who benefit are not necessarily those who suffered. Say, for instance, that an American law school may want to give special financial help for black students, because of past discrimination and a concern for the future racial balance of the legal profession. This may be a way of encouraging many to overcome social obstacles to education. Yet if the policy were to be operated on a purely racial basis, it would be totally blind to individual need. A rich black student might get free tuition, while many white students struggle to make ends meet, and some may be excluded altogether by poverty. In this case, a major distinction is being made on the basis of the colour of skin, and it could be argued that the same racial discrimination is operating as was the cause of so much suffering. The difference is now that it is being used to help. Colour of skin is still being made to matter. Whenever, however, groups are dealt with collectively, there will always be injustice to individuals whose needs are being ignored.

A Case History: American Law

The issue becomes particularly sensitive when admissions to professions such as law are at stake. A legal training in the United States is not just important for its own sake, but opens many doors to leadership. As the US Supreme Court pointed out in its judgment in 2003 on *Grutter* v. *Bollinger*, 'Individuals with law degrees occupy roughly half the state governorships, more than half the seats in the United States Senate, and more than a third of the seats in the United States House of Representatives.'[6] The Court comments that the pattern is even more striking if one looks at the influence of highly selective law schools. This argument about who goes to law school becomes a question of who is going to lead the country. There is, too, clearly a considerable political interest in encouraging diversity not just for its own sake, but for the importance of producing role models.

The case concerned the policy of the Law School of the University of Michigan.[7] The Law School wanted to achieve racial and ethnic diversity, 'with special reference to the inclusion of groups which have been historically discriminated against, like African-Americans, Hispanics and Native Americans, who without this commitment might not be represented in our student body in meaningful numbers'. Yet the school's case was that they wanted students who brought a different perspective to the law school, and that they were not intending to remedy past discrimination. The Supreme Court held, five to four, that the law school has a compelling interest in attaining a diverse student body, and that this can justify using race in university admissions.

One immediate question is, of course, what is meant by 'diverse'. If the idea is that there must be diversity of races, it is hard not to see an element of racial discrimination creeping back in, whatever the motive. Even the process of classifying races in the first place can be highly questionable. In Britain, 'Asians' are often grouped together, in ways that lump people of very different traditions together. Indians and Pakistanis are cheerfully treated as identical in ways that ignore highly significant religious and political differences. When leaders of the 'Asian community' are invoked, it may matter very much whether they are Hindus or Muslims (let alone Chinese). The same problem arises in deciding how to classify 'underrepresented minorities'. In a dissenting opinion on *Grutter* v. *Bollinger,* Justice Kennedy quoted evidence that faculty members could be 'breathtakingly cynical' about what counted as a relevant minority.[8] In a debate on whether Cubans were to be treated as Hispanics, a professor objected on the ground that the Cubans were Republicans. There is, though, a serious point here. If diversity of experience is the aim, there are many different ways of classifying minorities, and plenty of room for doubt about where to place individuals. Would someone with a Native American grandmother count as Native American? Where does one draw lines? There is often too quick an assumption that race is clear-cut, so that either one is of a particular race or one is not. Why, too, should race be the only issue in seeking diversity? What about political views? Ought we to be concerned at any underrepresentation by Republicans among the student body (and perhaps even more among faculty)? In the end, assigning individuals to categories may itself be somewhat arbitrary.

It is all too easy to assume that race always carries with it particular experiences and outlooks, and the stress on diversity does this. Otherwise it becomes a mere aesthetic demand. In dissent, Justice Thomas caustically accuses the law school of simply wanting to have a certain appearance, 'from the shape of the desks and tables in its classrooms to the color of the students sitting at them'.[9] In contrast, the court majority declares that 'just as growing up in a particular region or having particular professional experience is likely to affect an individual's views, so, too, is one's own, unique experience of being in a racial minority in a society, like our own, in which race, unfortunately, still matters'. Such a view tends to assume that race, and certain personal characteristics, must go together. How far this is true can be a matter for debate, but one thing is certain. As long as such a view is held, race will undoubtedly be made to matter.

The Supreme Court is, however, in no doubt that the US Constitution's guarantee of equal protection of the laws to each person protects individuals, and not groups.[10] Giving benefits to someone because of race might appear to ignore this. Indeed, in a judgment given the same day as *Grutter*, the court in *Gratz* v. *Bollinger*, dealing with the admissions policies of another part of the University of Michigan, was at pains for this reason to stress the importance of dealing with applications on an individual basis. It objected to the policy of automatically giving twenty points (one-fifth of the points needed to guarantee admission) to every single applicant from 'an underrepresented minority' group, as defined by the university.[11] This meant that individuals were assessed as representatives of a group, and not as individuals. Their own particular qualities were not assessed, and the mechanized index score decided the admissions decision in each case. Other factors, besides academic performance, could also give points, and such factors as residence in Michigan, being children of alumni or being recruited for athletics could also play a part. In a meritocratic society, of course, it could be queried whether these categories are any more relevant than race. Certainly they would not be regarded as relevant for admission to a British university. However, the point at issue before the court was possible violation of the Equal Protection Clause through classifications made on the basis of race, not what Justice Thomas referred to as 'arbitrary admissions procedures'. He suggested that the whole process is 'poisoned by numerous exceptions to "merit"'.[12] The objection to such exceptions is the moral one that people are being judged not because of their own abilities, but, say, because of who their parents are. They may not be judged by membership of a group, but considerations are entering that may not be morally relevant, and are thus open to similar objections. Justice Thomas, indeed, allows himself to point out a possible connection. Some may realize that forbidding racial discrimination in admissions may also encourage resistance to giving preference to the children of alumni.

The court believed that, in the law school case, diversity brought important educational benefits, and that this justified using race as a factor in making decisions about admissions. There was no quota system, and the court was assured that the admissions programme ensured that each applicant was reviewed as an individual, so that race or ethnicity was not a defining feature. All the ways in which a candidate might contribute to a diverse educational environment were taken into account. Thus it appeared that individuals were treated as such and not as members of a group. There was no mechanistic process of racial preference. Yet at the same time membership of a race was accepted as a relevant factor. Just how uncomfortable the court was in making this decision can be judged by its statement: 'We expect that 25 years from now, the use of racial preferences will no longer be necessary to further the interest approved today.'[13] Yet why something can be legally (and presumably morally) acceptable now, but not at another time, is not clear. It makes it look as if the decision is meant to meet a particular political situation, and is not itself a principled one. Certainly Justice Thomas is of that view, holding that the law school currently violates the Equal Protection Clause 'and that the Constitution means the same thing today as it will in 300 months'.[14]

In the end, however, this should not just be a legal matter, because it affects the basis of our moral thinking. Treating people differently because of the group they are assigned to cannot be just, whether it benefits them or not. Justice Thomas, who is himself black, stresses the central point when he says that 'the majority of blacks are admitted to the Law School because of discrimination, and because of this policy all are tarred as undeserving'. It gives a stigma both to those who have been admitted unfairly and to those who would still have succeeded without special preference, and without racial discrimination. He movingly quotes Frederick Douglass speaking in 1865 to a group of those supporting the abolition of slavery. Douglass said: 'What I ask for the Negro is not benevolence, not pity, not sympathy, but simply *justice*. The American people have always been anxious to know what they shall do with us. . . . I have had but one answer from the beginning. Do nothing with us! Your doing with us has already played the mischief with us.'[15]

Racial discrimination is not the only form of discrimination found objectionable. Other groups, sometimes self-defined, are ready to see themselves as victims, and allege unfair discrimination. Elderly people might be an example. Parallels are also drawn explicitly between discrimination on grounds of race, and discrimination because of sexual orientation. Certainly it is routine for institutions to make it their policy that they will not discriminate on grounds of sexual orientation. Often this is an application of the principle that we have already discussed, that people should not be judged because of the way they are classified, or because of their perceived membership of a group. Individuals should be seen as such, and not treated collectively. Otherwise one can get to the position reached by an ignorant mob in one English town. They were demonstrating against child abuse, and attacked the house of a children's doctor, under the misapprehension that a paediatrician was a paedophile.

These are complicated and sensitive matters, but one immediate issue is the connection between 'orientation' and practice. The fact that I have certain desires does not necessary mean that I should act on them. It may be an important matter for morality how far desires are fixed, or can be changed. Yet even if they are unalterable, it is hard to hold that they automatically drive us to act, unless one subscribes to a crude determinism. We have a choice, and in many areas of life, not just the sexual, we can be criticized from a moral standpoint for giving in to impulses. It is not a good idea to hit someone every time we lose our temper. Yet it is not clear sometimes whether the prohibition on discrimination means that there can be no moral criticism of what people actually do, particularly when this is affecting others adversely. People's actions are usually morally relevant.

People's innermost desires, making up their sexual orientation, are private and personal. This can make it appear that they are out of the public domain, in the sense that other people should not criticize them, or any actions they prompt. There is the distinction between what can be the subject of public discussion and what cannot be, and is thus 'private'. Yet there is also a less sophisticated sense of 'private', which just means that something is secret and difficult to detect. Sexual desires are indeed so private that those who have them may be unwilling to admit that they do, even to themselves. One does not need to be a psychoanalyst to realize that self-deception in such matters is rife, and that, in Freudian terms, desires can be 'repressed'. Unless, therefore, 'orientation' issues in action, it is sometimes hard to pin down.

All this may not seem to matter if one adopts a liberal position that says that sexual conduct is an individual choice, and of no concern to anyone else. This is to go from the privacy of innermost desires to a sense of privacy, which, as we have seen, can become ethical subjectivism. Whatever I want to do is then right for me. No doubt some of the passion in defending people's rights to various sexual orientations can stem from such a position. Yet very few people would want to go that far. There exists an association dedicated to the furtherance of 'man–boy love'. No doubt its members would claim that they have an orientation specifically directed to young boys. Others may find themselves attracted to young girls. Those who advocate paedophilia could claim that it springs from sexual orientation. Is it not then discrimination to refuse to employ such a person? Yet even liberals would accept that an institution caring for children should not employ someone who explicitly makes children sexual targets. The liberal objection may centre on the inability of a child to give informed consent, but it would still find paedophilia (or even its possibility) morally objectionable.

Another example where even the most liberal approach to sexuality would draw a line is rape. Again there is by definition a lack of consent. Yet a rapist might argue that his desires spring from a deep sexual orientation, which demands violence as an intrinsic part of what he wanted. It could surely be no defence for him that in taking action, society is 'discriminating against' his sexual orientation. He is not being treated as a member of a group, but is himself being held responsible for the harm he has himself caused.

These examples suggest that an unwillingness to put people into arbitrary groups, and use that as a basis for unjust treatment, should not be confused with the claim that all sexual behaviour is somehow immune from criticism. The reason for outlawing unjust discrimination is seeing people as individuals who are responsible for their own actions, not as ciphers defined by some racial, class or other social category. Yet once 'sexual orientation' is acted on, it is inevitably the responsibility of the agent. Paedophiles should not escape responsibility for what they do, behind blanket prohibitions on discrimination by the rest of us, any more than the label 'paedophile' should be flung around in a hysterical fashion to blacken the characters of innocent people. In this case, as in others, arbitrary classifications can prove the antithesis of justice.

Notes

1 Alan M. Dershowitz, *Why Terrorism Works: Understanding the Threat, Responding to Its Challenge*, Yale University Press, New Haven, CT, 2002, p. 117.

2 Amy Gutmann, 'Responding to racial injustice', in K. Anthony Appiah and Amy Gutmann, *Color Conscious: The Political Morality of Race*, Princeton University Press, Princeton, NJ, 1996, p. 179.

3 Ibid., p. 148.

4 Ibid., p. 170.

5 Ibid., p. 175.

6 *Grutter* v. *Bollinger*, 539, US 306, 123 S.Ct 2325, 2341, 156, L.Ed.2d 304 (2003).

7 *Grutter*, at 2331.

8 *Grutter*, at 2372 (Kennedy J., dissenting).

9 *Grutter*, at 2352 n3 (Thomas J., dissenting).

10 *Grutter*, at 2337.

11 *Gratz* v. *Bollinger*, 539 US 244, 123 S.Ct 2411, 2427–8,156 L.Ed.2d 257 (2003).

12 *Grutter*, at 2359 (Thomas J., dissenting).

13 *Grutter*, at 2347.

14 *Grutter*, at 2351 (Thomas J., dissenting).

15 *Grutter*, at 2350 (Thomas J., dissenting).

8

Patriotism and nationalism

The Dangers of Patriotism

Moral distinctions should not be made because of arbitrary classifications on the basis of a group. Racism is objectionable because of this. Yet what about citizenship of a country? How morally relevant is that? Many may think they have a special affinity with, and responsibility for, their fellow citizens. They take it for granted that they should be more concerned with their fellow citizens, and their needs, than with people at the other end of the earth. Yet some would think that being British or American is as morally irrelevant as being white or black.

Every September at the end of the summer season of Promenade Concerts in the Royal Albert Hall, London, a concert is given, on 'The Last Night of the Proms'. It has developed into a major event, which, after a sober first half of classical music, ends with the enthusiastic singing of patriotic songs. There is much waving of flags, and a good time is had by all. Every year, however, there is embarrassment, expressed in the press, at the open display of patriotic emotion, and judgements are passed about its dangers. Other countries, too, express their patriotism. Americans are very ready to fly their flag outside their houses, particularly when they feel a need to show national unity. Yet some see sinister overtones in the display of flags, and in more significant displays of patriotism. Memories of the nationalism of Nazi Germany can be rekindled. One has only to see the rival displays of flags, and symbols, marking out the respective territories of different communities in a divided city such as Belfast to see the incipient danger.

There is clearly a moral problem here. Loyalty to a country, or a community, has often been portrayed as an elevated human trait. Yet the very idea implies an exclusivity, which dismisses those beyond as less important. Membership of a country, however, may give us our identity, both individually and collectively. It has certainly helped to mould us. Do we not in turn owe it loyalty? This moral claim may be more striking when we think of the plight of stateless refugees. Given the way human life is currently arranged, nations, or, at least, states (and the two may not be the same), provide an indispensable backdrop for human life. Without the protection of a particular citizenship, we are cast adrift. Indeed, sometimes that may literally be the case, as when refugees in boats find that no country will accept them.

In return for the provision of protection, and additional benefits, such as education, health care and general social welfare, citizens may be deemed to have an obligation to help the state in its task. They owe it their trust and support. No state can exist without its citizens. One of the dangers inherent in the glorification of any state is that it may take on a life of its own, which seems to exist apart from the lives of its members. This can lead to a personification of the state, and a suppression of individual interest in favour of some abstract conception of what is necessary for the whole. That is the path of oppression, since the interests of a state cannot run counter to those of its citizens. If they all seek a self-sacrificial death to uphold the glory of the fatherland, there may be a question as to what is going to be left. There may be many things worth fighting for, but the glory of an abstraction may not be one of them.

We have already noted that states, as political entities, may not be the same as 'nations'. Loyalty to a nation, which is not politically organized, can create powerful emotions, and can lead to political upheavals, fracturing existing states. When political boundaries fail to reflect the self-understanding of citizens, there can be trouble. Language, tradition, religion or territorial identity (as with an island) may all serve to fuel people's desire to see themselves as separate. When some do desire this, and others alongside them do not, there are the seeds of a nasty civil war. The apparent imposition of an alien religion or language, or the enforced allegiance to particular traditions and history, can lead to violence. The continuing tug between the two communities in Ireland, each proud of its history, is only one example of a widespread problem.

Yet even if we accept the existing framework of states, and ignore the nationalism that can so easily subvert them, it can be argued that the mere existence of states contributes to the troubles of the world. They threaten each other, and go to war with each other. The history of the twentieth

century in Europe provided an unsavoury succession of power struggles and
animosities, which twice ignited world war. Millions have died as a result.
The urge behind the formation of the European Union, and its attempts to
achieve 'ever closer union', has very largely been a desire to put an end to
European wars, by reducing the role of the separate states. Although it could
be viewed as a step to a world government, it could also just become a
superstate. How far nationalist passions within Europe can be weakened
remains to be seen. Certainly there is a potential for bigger confrontations,
and bigger power struggles on a global scale, perhaps for reasons of trade.
The enemies may change, but the fact of conflict may not.

States, whether great or small, may be necessary, but their existence can be
the source of great problems. Given this, should we take pride in our
allegiance to one? Love of country seems to be very deeply rooted in
human arrangements. Political systems often deliberately encourage it
through education. The delight in the familiar, and the affection for what is
ours, is so pervasive that it seems basic in human nature. From the moral
point of view, is this good or bad? Is it really right to prefer one set of humans
to another? It may seem morally dubious to devote our energies in a selective
manner to one place and not another.

The Limits of Moral Concern

Any moral view which stresses the relevance of human nature is drawn to
the conclusion that it should be concerned with all humans, from wherever
they come. It could be argued that moral progress has consisted in the
growing realization that we have obligations to all, regardless of race,
country or other allegedly irrelevant factor. Greater moral understanding,
it may be held, leads us away from a preoccupation with families, kin or
nation. We have, it seems, to recognize a common humanity as the root of
moral claims, even when shared by people who appear very unlike us. Our
ambit of concern has gradually widened to encompass all humans. The
abolition of the slave trade stemmed from a recognition that racial differences were not morally relevant. Unfair treatment of women has to be
challenged because our humanity, and not our sex, is seen as morally crucial.
We all share the same basic needs.

The dilemma in all this is clear. Once a common humanity is stressed,
how can I go on favouring those who belong to my country, at the expense

of those who live beyond its borders? Martha Nussbaum has written, about the widening of compassion from our parochial setting, that 'for many Americans, that expansion of moral concern stops at the national boundary'.[1] The same could be said, no doubt, about the inhabitants of other countries. We care most about what happens to those near us. By extension this can be extended to others like us, who share our traditions and customs. The difficulty comes in an idea of an expanding circle of concern which takes in those who not only are unrelated, but cannot affect us in any way. We have already referred to the biological categories of kin selection and reciprocal altruism, which are used by neo-Darwinians to show the biological roots of morality. Our children, who are likely to share the same genes, are not likely to survive to spread them if we do not look after them. Thus love of family will have genetic roots if anything does, because our genes will be winnowed out of the gene pool if we do not care for those who share them. Similarly, the argument is that those who cooperate with others, at least up to a point, are more likely to do well. We gain biological advantage by helping those who may help us in return. Both of these categories deal with people with whom we are in contact, and who can affect us. Neither, by definition, can apply to anyone who is unrelated to us, or who can have no effect on our lives. The implication is that, if this account of genetic transmission is correct and if morality only springs from biology, morality cannot involve abstractions like 'humanity'. It can only deal with those with whom we have some kind of direct relationship.

Many, in contrast, believe that morality and altruism must be intimately connected. Altruism cannot be qualified, but in its genuine form it involves offering assistance and meeting the needs of others, with no thought of gain and no automatic pay-off. It gives disinterested help even to those who are in no position to reciprocate. It is not like mutual grooming in apes. While, therefore, some of our impulses to help others may have biological roots, the kind of people we may feel naturally inclined to help will be rather limited. Neo-Darwinians would expect to find an ingrained preference for family, and also a desire to help those whose destiny and well-being is bound up with our own. Yet what happens when an expanding ambit of concern becomes universal? Why should we expend effort, at great cost to ourselves, in helping those who will not be able to provide us even with any indirect benefits? If we accept the doctrines of evolutionary biology we may feel that the claims of our common humanity may not make much headway. An innate desire to help our family and further our own interests, through cooperating with those who may be important in helping us, may seem to dominate.

There is an even deeper question that must be faced. Is it even a good thing, from a moral point of view, that we should value all human beings equally? Many would be horrified at parents who made no distinction between their own children and those of others. There seems something morally repugnant, as well as unnatural, about those who expend more effort obtaining food for starving children on the other side of the world than in feeding their own children. One could also imagine doctors, or aid workers, caught with a family in the midst of terrible deprivation, and being faced with the problem of whether to make an exception in favour of their own children. How far should they be ready to save them at the expense of others? We might admire those who were prepared to go hungry themselves to help others, but would we equally admire those who treated their own children as just some of many in equal need? At the very least, there would appear to be an agonizing moral dilemma in such cases.

The morality of generalized concern and a universal love of humanity is in sharp contrast to the neo-Darwinian view of morality growing out of an animal inheritance favouring kin. The former condemns 'nepotism', while the latter sees the source and power of morality as growing out of basic feelings of attachment to family. The one is highly rational, while the other is more a matter of emotion. The problem with the rational picture is that a generalized love of, and respect for, humanity is all very well, but it is meaningless unless cashed out in concern for real people. There are some who espouse high-minded concern for humanity, fighting for peace and against poverty. The only trouble is that, when they stop fighting for causes, and deal with real people, they can be unscrupulous, manipulative and utterly selfish. On the other side, someone could be loving to family and caring of close friends, but deaf to the claims of those beyond. Dictators have been known for their happy family life and love of children. That has not prevented them wreaking havoc on the world and making millions suffer.

Emotions lose their strength as their objects become general or abstract. It is harder to have an emotional attachment to humanity than to individuals. The picture of a widening circle of concern often carries the implication that such concern becomes attenuated and weakened the further it is stretched from our immediate situation. This is the danger of resting morality on basic impulses of affection or primitive feelings of solidarity with those with whom we identify. A biological account of love of kindred will find it hard to account for loyalty to a large community. Frans de Waal is well known for his studies of what he sees as the biological roots of morality, as shown in ape behaviour. He remarks:

Human sympathy is not unlimited. It is offered most readily to one's own family and clan, less readily to other members of the community, and, most reluctantly, if at all, to outsiders. The same is true of the succorant behavior of animals. The two share not only a cognitive and emotional basis, therefore, but similar constraints on their expression.[2]

We may, as a result, be able to identify more easily with a locality in which we know many people and regularly interact with them. We may see the advantages of mutual agreements covering larger numbers, in part because of the benefits size can bring. We may be better defended by a larger army. There must, however, came a point at which the scale of political organization runs the risk that its members lose a feeling of identity with it. Even the size of a democracy can prohibit mutual discussion and negotiation, which is the very stuff of democracy. Then we elect representatives to negotiate for us, but a gap can then open up between 'us' and 'them', legislators and citizens, which itself can inhibit feelings of loyalty and identity.

Particular and Universal Loyalties

Modern states may be bigger than biological impulses can cope with. Yet we do still wish to belong somewhere, and identify with, and cooperate with, those around us. Political organizations can exploit these urges. When we step beyond allegiance to country, we find ourselves having to appeal to abstractions such as humanity. We are involved in pleas for equality and universal justice. Not only is it sometimes hard to see any emotional appeal in such things. They involve claims which may actually run counter to our biological inheritance, rather than make use of it. Altruists are often, in biological terms, regarded as pursuing a doomed policy. By incurring costs to help others, they make it harder for their genes to be passed on. It seems as if a gene to encourage pure altruism could never be consistently transmitted through the generations. It belongs to biological losers, and not winners. Is altruism therefore impossible? The answer must be that it seems to be, if we think that morality is powerless when faced with our undoubtedly influential biological inheritance. Who we help may not, though, be just a matter of who we naturally identify with. We can surely use our reason, as well our 'gut impulses'. We may be able to go beyond them. We may even be able to control them when they seem particularly dangerous.

These problems have been well illustrated by Martha Nussbaum. She argues that an emphasis on patriotic pride is morally dangerous.[3] She contrasts loyalty to country with the application of universal moral standards, saying that she wants to put in the place of the patriot 'the very old ideal of the cosmopolitan, the person whose allegiance is to the worldwide community of human beings'. Her position is that 'to give support to nationalist sentiments subverts, ultimately, even the values that hold a nation together, because it substitutes a colorful idol for the substantive universal values of justice and right'.[4] Her creed is that 'we should recognize humanity, wherever it occurs, and give its fundamental ingredients, reason and moral capacity, our first allegiance and respect'. She accepts that we need not give up our special affections and identifications, 'whether ethnic or gender-based or religious'.[5] Our main efforts, however, should be devoted to concern for all human beings. Our particular identities may be tolerated, but hardly cherished. The kind of patriotism that induces people to put a sticker on their cars saying 'Proud to be an American' elicits little encouragement from her. It is, she would think, dangerous and constricting, because it encourages a restriction of sympathies, and is an obstacle to the recognition of humanity as such. It could, the charge would run, encourage a feeling of Americans against the rest. In those circumstances, being 'un-American' is a more serious accusation than being 'inhuman'.

The ease with which Nussbaum passes from talking about 'patriotism' to referring to 'nationalist sentiments' suggests that she does not see any distinction between the two. Her belief that we should be citizens of the world may lead her to ignore significant differences. A patriot may certainly have a love of country, but it need not be a love that shuts out the rest of the world, let alone subordinates everything to the interests of one nation. A patriot can recognize that those who are loyal to other countries can also be patriots. The fact that I love my country may enable me to recognize and respect your equal love for yours. Nationalists, however, will be more aggressive in pursuing the interests of their country above all others. Aggrandizement and power will be the objects, and this may well involve conflict and subjugation. Nationalists can easily turn to violence and terror in pursuit of their goals. They would not allow their national pretensions to be held back by appeals to universal justice, even if, paradoxically, their nationalism can often be fuelled by a powerful sense of injustice.

Patriotism may engender deep emotion, but the question is whether love of country undermines a concern for universal justice. True patriotism, it could be claimed, may focus moral claims, while not being exclusive. Indeed, far from it being a 'colourful idol', it may help us to see that that we have a duty to others. The idea of loyalty to a country itself makes use of that of moral obligation. It gives a particular expression to the idea of serving others, which must surely play a central role in any morality. Charles Taylor says: 'The societies we are striving to create – free, democratic, willing to some degree to share equally – require strong identification on the part of their citizens.'[6] Societies do not acquire these characteristics easily, since they involve compromise and cooperation. They have to counteract ingrained human selfishness. Notions of loyalty to something valuable beyond oneself can only help in this task.

The dilemma is always the tug between particular loyalties, and the recognition of universal obligations. Love of country can shut out, both literally and figuratively, those beyond its borders. Yet a general benevolence for humanity may by its very generality lose the power to enthuse and motivate. Further, it does not seem to provide any obvious starting point for action. The world is full of the needy. Where should we start? The result could be a mixture of pious platitudes and frozen indecision. By beginning with those nearest to us, at least we know who we should be helping. We can learn our obligations near at home. The problem is how we can extend them.

Martha Nussbaum does agree with this. She says that 'politics, like child care, would be poorly done, if each thinks herself equally responsible for all, rather than giving the immediate surroundings special attention and care'.[7] Yet we still need a motive for doing so, especially if there is a cost. Natural sympathies may help, but are not necessarily reliable. This is where the moral basis of a genuine patriotism should come into its own. It should give us reasons for caring for those for whom we have a particular responsibility. Otherwise, without particular obligations, everyone will leave it to everyone else. Someone in trouble is much less likely to receive help in a crowded city street than in a quiet country lane. When I am the only person available, I am much more likely to do something than when a hundred others could also help. A general concern must always be supplemented by the recognition of a specific need for action.

No moral claim can be discussed in isolation from issues of responsibility. It is no good saying that something should be done, without having some idea of who should do it. Aristotle saw that, when property was held in common, no one would take care of it, since it was not theirs. No one had any special responsibility for it. He advocated private property, and was opposed to Plato's ideal state, which held property in common. In addition,

Aristotle was deeply opposed to a state which did not uphold family life, but (as in Plato's *Republic*) held women and children in common. In a trenchant phrase, he said that in those circumstances, 'love will be watery'.[8] He points out that a father would not say 'my son', or the son 'my father'. He explains: 'As a little sweet wine mingled with a great deal of water is imperceptible in the mixture, so, in this sort of community, the idea of relationship which is based upon these names will be lost: there is no reason why the so-called father should care about the son, or the son about the father, or brothers about one another.'

Aristotle hammers the point home by stressing how important for establishing affection is the simple idea that a thing is one's own. If something is mine, I am responsible for it, since no one else will take it or look after it. The point remains whether it is a prized bicycle given to a boy for his birthday, or a loved child, an object or a person. Affection, pride and responsibility are bound together. So it must be with countries. Unless citizens think in terms of 'their' country, they will not be able to identify with it and care for it, even to the point of self-sacrifice. Yet those who see themselves as cosmopolitans will say that that is what they are afraid of. Identification with a country may generate a form of moral commitment, and feelings of responsibility, in a way that can threaten others. It seems that the issue is not the fact of our loyalty, but the nature of the society which receives it. Unless it is to become dangerous, patriotism must be harnessed to a country which itself encapsulates, and encourages, the very highest moral ideals.

Nationalism can demand a loyalty to a state which recognizes no power or authority beyond itself. Its members will only be concerned with its interests, and it will be impatient with a patriotism that accepts moral constraints. In other words, the state will become an end in itself. The true patriot, on the other hand, may be motivated by love of country, but could simultaneously see it as an instrument for spreading justice and other universal values. One could love one's country precisely because one sees it as a part of a moral crusade. Many will be unhappy with this thought. The word 'crusade' carries with it historical reverberations suggesting the imposition of the moral standards, and even the religion, of one country on those who have no wish to share them. Yet this view can lead straight to relativism, and a denial that conventions in one place have any bearing on what should happen in another. Intriguingly, those who talk of being citizens of the world do so precisely because they are not relativists, and accept universal standards.

Liberals are often suspicious of patriotism, not least because patriots have deep commitments to particular conceptions of what is good. The point of liberalism, as, for instance, adumbrated by John Rawls, is that the state should not take sides in debates between citizens about what is good. It certainly, therefore, should not embody a particular moral vision in its dealings with other states. Anthony Appiah writes in this context of 'the respect for the autonomy of individuals, which resists the state's desire to fit us to someone else's conception of what is good for us'.[9] Liberalism goes together with a stress on the role of the individual in deciding what is good. This is going to be at odds with a patriotism that sees a country as the vehicle of values to which one should be committed. This can degenerate into a devotion to my country 'right or wrong', but that actually merges with relativism, because in practice it fails to accept that my country could be wrong. Its standards are then the only possible ones for its members, even if not for others. At its best, however, the idea of a country as the bearer of moral standards points to moral truths which apply everywhere. In case this degenerates into arrogance, it should always be borne in mind that a country can be mistaken about what is true, as much as any individual. There is always scope for humility at both the personal and the national level.

Liberals are often very reluctant to make claims which suggest that others are mistaken. Because of their passionate commitment to autonomy, they want to tolerate, and even encourage, diversity and difference. Yet Appiah, after talking of individual autonomy, goes on to complete a list of what he supposes is 'at the heart of liberal theory' by upholding 'the notion of human rights – rights possessed by human beings as such'.[10] Such a notion, however important, must restrict ideals of human autonomy and, even more, ideals of the autonomy of states. They are not free to decide that human rights do not matter. No liberal, therefore, can consistently condemn a patriot merely on the ground of upholding a substantive moral position. Patriots may hold that their country should encourage and live by a particular ethical view. Cosmopolitans may think a country has no significant role in the transmission of morality. The question, however, then arises as to where cosmopolitan ideals come from. By definition, it seems, they could not have been nurtured in the soil of any particular environment. Yet the danger is that self-proclaimed cosmopolitans apply standards that must have taken root at a particular place and time, without caring about their origin. The standards may certainly have a universal claim. The problem is, though, that cosmopolitans may feel little emotional attachment to a particular place or tradition. Yet their ideas have come from somewhere, even if they choose not to acknowledge that fact.

Human reason may break free of its social context, but it is idle to pretend that there is not one. Only relativists believe that reason is constituted and defined by its social setting. Yet only the most optimistic product of the European Enlightenment could imagine that our ways of reasoning do not themselves have histories. The American philosopher Hilary Putnam uses a point often made in the philosophy of science, when he points out to Nussbaum that reason never operates in a vacuum. We have to start from somewhere. He believes that ideas of justice, and other moral claims, are rooted in ways of life. He pithily claims: 'Tradition without reason is blind; reason without tradition is empty.'[11] Even modern science is built on the shoulders of earlier scientists, and depends on a powerful tradition.

The cosmopolitan vision needs to recognize its dependency on tradition. A patriotism with a moral vision is not so very different from the cosmopolitan appeal to human rights and universal moral claims. They each articulate a powerful morality. One relates it to the local situation of a particular country, but is willing to look outside. The other pretends it has no roots. Yet if it is to be effective, it has to start from somewhere, and be applied somewhere first. Perhaps it is necessary for anyone with an idea of what is morally important from the world standpoint to start from where they are. They should attempt to make their own country, whether it is their native one or adopted, a moral agent in bringing about a state of affairs that reflects universal standards of justice. Many will still be afraid that mention of a particular country will encourage an exclusivity that sees national boundaries as morally significant. The worry is that whereas 'charity begins at home' may be a good patriotic creed, all too often charity stays there.

Many will also be concerned about viewing the state as itself some kind of moral agent, instead of as a neutral umpire refusing to be aligned with any particular morality. There could be many significant consequences, not least the encouragement of an official culture, which would itself influence the education system. The patriot may believe that a particular country embodies a moral outlook, which should be passed on to future generations. As a result, the state may wish to promote a distinctive culture as the national culture, and give a very specific content to public moral education. Yet this immediately raises the question of 'indoctrination' and the right of individuals to live their own lives, even in a manner many would disapprove of. The liberal state would find indoctrination repugnant, but, as we have seen before, liberalism is itself a distinctive ideal, and that itself has to be taught. The question then becomes not whether morality should be passed on, but what kind of morality should be. Even neutrality in education about moral concerns, on the grounds that they are issues for personal choice, can send a powerful message. It can appear that because they are private and not public, they do not matter from a public point of view. Neutrality can look like indifference. The absence of moral teaching can itself be morally influential.

The Patriot and the Cosmopolitan

There is still likely to be a clash between those who see a particular responsibility to those around us, and those who see justice as totally impartial. As we have seen, many do not see love of country, and feelings of affinity to one's fellow citizens, as even desirable. They would certainly not wish to encourage them in schools. They are afraid of any distinctions being indicated between the familiar and the alien, the citizen and the foreigner. Nationalists will not be too concerned about this kind of moral disagreement, since they are primarily interested in power. Patriots and cosmopolitans may have competing visions, but they both make moral claims. It is unfair to suggest that cosmopolitans love universal justice, while patriots do not. The former do not believe that a particular country can be the focus of moral conviction. Its very particularity seems too restrictive and exclusive. Yet patriots who see their country as the context in which morality can be practised and transmitted would not wish to limit the reach of morality. They would see their country, at its best, as a force for good beyond its borders. Love of country would be an enabling factor, in the spread of a moral vision, and the means of discharging special responsibilities to those near us. Despite the fears of many, it need not, and should not, ignore the needs of others.

Yet many may still be worried. Once it is accepted that a society has to transmit a moral vision through the generations, the charge will be that this is bound to breed exclusivity. One of the reasons, indeed, why there is opposition in so many countries to immigration is that there is fear of a dilution of a particular culture. Some would claim that this could take even more emphatic, and unpleasant, forms if it is accepted that culture includes morality. There may therefore appear to be moral grounds for setting up barriers to outsiders, so as to preserve a moral inheritance. Morality, it seems, can then be used as a pretext for treatment that on most views must be regarded as immoral.

There may well be a difference in emphasis between patriot and cosmopolitan, but their views may not be as antagonistic as they might first appear. A cosmopolitan may set no great store by national boundaries, and see no reason for anything but absolute freedom to cross borders. Patriots may worry that their country, and all it stands for, could be changed beyond recognition. Yet the cosmopolitan love of freedom, and respect for individuals, has to be learnt somewhere. There has to be a certain kind of moral and political background for such views to make sense, and to be able to gain any purchase. In the same way, patriots may well hold that the morality of their country encourages precisely the love of freedom, and respect for all people, that the cosmopolitan requires.

Immigration can bring many practical problems, the most obvious being the possibility of overcrowding. The moral issues are, however, less intractable. Few patriots would turn away those who would return to certain death in their own country. Few cosmopolitans would welcome newcomers who were intent on destroying the freedom they hold dear. Yet there are still arguments about the effect of immigration on culture, including traditional morality. The difference, in this respect, between patriot and cosmopolitan may simply lie in the fact that a patriot may recognize the fragility of moral traditions. A cosmopolitan may be more optimistic about the robustness of a love of freedom, and other moral impulses. A possible danger in a belief in universal values can be that there is too easy a slide from asserting that they have a claim on everyone to the view that they are in fact going to be recognized by everyone. Perhaps there is a danger in being too optimistic about people's natural inclinations to altruism. Some do not take seriously enough the difficulties of teaching, and preserving, the moral standards they recognize.

It is a strength of patriotism, at its best, that it recognizes that the state, like other institutions such as the family, has an indispensable moral function. One's country can be a force for good, and for the transmission of a belief in what is good. When things go wrong, as in Hitler's Germany, they can go very wrong, and true patriots may well find that, for their country's sake, they have to resist a particular regime. One cannot, though, escape this possibility by pretending that one's country means nothing in the first place. It is doubtful whether human motivation can be harnessed, and loyalty stimulated, by the impersonal abstractions of appeals to justice. It is claimed that 'our primary moral allegiance is to no community...our primary allegiance is to justice'.[12] This may make sense as a theoretical remark by a philosopher, but it is doubtful whether it would enthuse many. It is precisely because our primary allegiance is to what is right and good that we should seek to serve our country to ensure that it always exemplifies the best standards in its collective life. Those who love justice, but fail to love their country, despite its many imperfections, could well be paying lip-service to a set of standards which are not really implemented in their lives.

Notes

1   Martha C. Nussbaum, 'Introduction', in *For Love of Country*, ed. Martha C. Nussbaum, Beacon Press, Boston, 2002, p. xii.
2   Frans de Waal, *Good-natured: The Origins of Right and Wrong in Humans and Other Animals*, Harvard University Press, Cambridge, MA, 1996, p. 88.
3   Martha C. Nussbaum, 'Patriotism and cosmopolitanism', in *For Love of Country*, p. 4.
4   Ibid., p. 5.
5   Ibid., p. 9.
6   Charles Taylor, 'Why democracy needs patriotism', in *For Love of Country*, p. 119.
7   Nussbaum, 'Patriotism and cosmopolitanism', p. 13.
8   Aristotle, *Politics*, 1262b (Book II, 4).
9   K. Anthony Appiah, 'Cosmopolitan patriots', in *For Love of Country*, p. 25.
10 Ibid.
11 Hilary Putnam, 'Must we choose?', in *For Love of Country*, p. 94.
12 Amy Gutmann, 'Democratic citizenship', in *For Love of Country*, p. 69.

9

One world: a global ethic?

A Cosmopolitan Law?

Arguments about patriotism soon lead to discussions about the necessity for a moral framework for the conduct of international affairs. We have obligations and responsibilities to our fellow citizens. We have a particular loyalty to our own country. Morality, however, does not stop there. Just as a proper love of family does not preclude responsibility for what happens to other people in our society, so patriotism cannot provide an excuse for ignoring the rest of the world. Human rights, for instance, are seen as universal. Thus John Rawls says: 'Human rights are a class of rights that play a special role in a reasonable Law of Peoples: they restrict the justifying reasons for war and its conduct, and they specify limits to a regime's internal autonomy.'[1] The hope is that nations can thus be restrained from some of the more horrendous aspects of modern warfare. Yet Rawls's mention of limits to autonomy challenges some ideas of national sovereignty. International affairs are a matter of the relationship of nations. The question is how far they are to be regarded as free agents, and in what sense they can be restricted by moral claims.

Rawls follows Kant, who believed that states may be judged 'like individual men'.[2] They injure each other when they are unrestrained by external laws, and therefore should be led to enter into a 'covenant of peoples'. Kant remarks that 'the violation of right in one place of the earth is felt in all places', and advocates a 'cosmopolitan law'.[3] He suggests that, far from being fantastic, it complements existing understandings of 'the law of the state and the law of nations'. He links the idea of an encompassing public law with the hope of 'eternal peace'. In this he was an apostle of the eighteenth-century Enlightenment, trusting in the power of rationality to come to significant ethical conclusions. Reason, for him, had to rise above the demands of our normal human impulses. Under its influence, progress was assured.

The history of the twentieth century made many despair of the use of reason to achieve a better world. Yet there is a continuing philosophical argument between those who wish to work with existing human sympathies and loyalties, and those who see them as the source of evil. Can we use our reason to start afresh, or do we accept human nature as it is, with all its tendencies and propensities? Should we follow existing traditions, some with a dubious history, or do we use our reason to build a better world from scratch?

There are connections with the argument between those who wish to see morality as universal, and those who relate morality to tradition and locality. The question is whether we follow the conventions of our particular tradition, or are subject to universal values applying to all nations. An Enlightenment belief in reason, like Kant's, might encourage many to think in terms of a 'cosmopolitan law'. They might look to an international arena, in which moral standards can be enforced on the behaviour of nations. Anyone wanting to uphold the interests of a particular nation would be seen, on the analogy with individuals, as enforcing 'selfish' standards. They would be like egoists, only at an international level. They may refuse to see any higher authority than their own local conventions. Democracy could even be seen as encouraging such relativism. If a nation's policy is to be rooted in the will of its people, and different nations express different wills, what different people agree in different places appears of paramount importance. Any international order based on an objective ethics would conflict with the idea of locally generated and agreed norms. Thus democracy and objective morality can become separated, just as international justice can appear opposed to local patriotism.

Democracy could be merely a matter of political agreement between individuals in a particular jurisdiction. It might create conventions but not be based on any prior shared moral understanding. Yet if morality is to be anything more than a shifting set of political agreements, it must provide standards against which the behaviour of nations, as well as of individuals, can be measured. Those who think that it is not enough to look after the interests of our own country inevitably look to a new global order. The temptation, however, is to see this in exclusively political terms. Wider moral concerns then seem to involve subscribing to the idea of an international government, so as to enforce a cosmopolitan law. It then appears that one has the choice either of giving priority to the interests of one's own country or of working for some new form of world politics.

Any embryonic world government must challenge the idea of national sovereignty. Building on the work of the United Nations, the idea is to give concrete form to an international morality. Morality, some think, cannot gain a grip in international relations if there are no institutions to regulate it. Universal moral laws are considered meaningless unless they are codified in an international law which is enforceable. Any idea of a covenant of peoples immediately suggests that there must be sanctions for those that break it, just as there are to ensure security within a society. The idea that people ought not be treated in certain ways evolves into the notion of crimes against humanity. The idea of a crime immediately carries with it the suggestion of a legal system which demarcates and prohibits certain behaviour as criminal. This then leads to the establishment of special courts to administer international justice. Morality is transmuted into politics, and the latter demands structures and institutions through which laws can be enforced.

The former British Prime Minister Margaret Thatcher notes that the setting up of the International Criminal Court at The Hague carries with it further implications. The United States has had grave objections to it, but it is now formally established. She points out: 'A global juridical institution of the kind proposed would require a global police force, and at least in embryo, a global government, in order to ensure that its decisions were actually carried out.'[4] She later remarks that the absence of any world police or army merely reflects that there can be no democratic legitimacy for them. She says: 'There is no world government, because there *is* no world 'nation', no world political identity, no world public opinion.'[5] No doubt many would retort that she is pursuing a nationalist agenda, which puts the interests of one nation above all ethical considerations.

There is seemingly an inexorable tug from the recognition of the importance of human rights, to their international enforcement, and onwards to the creation of the means to do so. This is in the name of universal moral principles. The particular views of a particular people can appear self-serving when judged against the universal claims of our common humanity. Institutions are thus advocated to express the latter, but can well clash with the democratically expressed will of particular societies. Yet the basic issue is not that of morality versus national interest, nor even the objectivity of morality against relativism. It is who is to decide the content of morality, and how, or whether, to enforce it. The objectivity of morality certainly entails the existence of a universal moral order which all should recognize. It does not necessarily mean that international, bureaucratic, organizations have to be set up to enforce it. Morality does not even have to be codified in a law of the land to demand our allegiance. Similarly, moral principles do not have to be codified in international law, let alone enforced globally by a world army, to be binding on us. It is a mistake to assume that morality, even the morality of nations, is only real if it takes on a political guise.

Democracy itself is predicated on the moral responsibility of citizens, and any policy which takes that away not only undermines democracy, but removes the possibility of free choice, and hence of moral agency. Whether or not international institutions should be set up to enforce a 'cosmopolitan law', governments ought to be answerable to the people they represent, and those people should never forget their moral responsibilities, any more than members of a government should. International agreement cannot manufacture morality. As with all agreements, it is a prior moral issue whether they are to be kept, in this case even when it is against a national interest. International agreements, like negotiations between individuals, depend on the underlying integrity and honesty of those who are party to them.

Morality can never be simply a matter of having the right institutions, and this applies in international relations as much as anywhere. All institutions depend on the commitment of their members in order to function. An international body to uphold human rights will only succeed if there is a will to respect human rights in the first place. Institutions can be important, but they themselves depend on individual morality. They do not replace it, let alone constitute it. Yet some would say this is too individualistic. Individuals and institutions are different, they will say, and operate differently. The one should not reduced to the other. Those acting in an official capacity on behalf of a country cannot behave as if they were private individuals. They cannot, it may be said, be governed by their own conscience, as they have specific responsibilities to discharge. Politicians, for instance, have special responsibilities to those they represent. If they do not put the interests of those they represent above those of people living on the other side of the world, they could be accused of not doing their job. It would be remarkable if they chose the interests of other countries rather than their own. That indeed is what a traitor does.

Perhaps relations between nations, as opposed to those between individuals, may not seem to fit easily into an ordinary moral framework. Some would say that the clash of nations is after all just a matter of power, and of the single-minded pursuit of national interest. Indeed, some politicians make it a

virtue that they are above all promoting the 'national interest'. A British Prime
Minister who defended the interests of French farmers to the detriment of
British ones would be seen as failing in his or her duty. Members of a
government, in other words, have a moral duty to look after those who
have elected them, in preference to others. They have been given specific
responsibilities, and if they do not fulfil them, it is unlikely others can. It is an
analogous position to that of parents who should care for their own children,
rather than other people's.

Global Responsibilities

Does a government not have responsibilities to people outside its jurisdiction? The question is the relevance of our common humanity, when weighed
against specific responsibilities to electors. Any democratic politician is
answerable to them, and may consider that aid to other nations, particularly
at great expense to one's own, may be electorally unpopular. On the other
hand, it may well be demanded by a public opinion shocked by television
pictures of suffering through famine or earthquake. Yet the question remains
as to whether a politician should just be governed by public opinion. In a
democratic society, it may perhaps be right that the will of the people
prevails, but this only pushes the question back a stage. Should ordinary
electors be concerned about what happens beyond their borders?

Such concern can sometimes be justified on prudential grounds. Kant's
reference to the violation of right being felt in all places may reflect this.
Injustice in one place can provoke reactions that spill over elsewhere. We all
have to face modern terrorism, which is liable to strike anywhere at any time
in the pursuit of causes thousands of miles away. Perhaps no one can hope to
remain unaffected even by occurrences in remote countries. National boundaries, too, no longer contain the effects of ordinary actions. Peter Singer
comments: 'That seemingly harmless and trivial human actions can affect
people in distant countries is just beginning to make a significant difference
to the sovereignty of individual nations.'[6] Pollution, and its possible long-
term effects on climate change, is a case in point. Even individual decisions
about driving a car to work, instead of using public transport, can, taken
together, affect the atmosphere, with unknown consequences.

Singer states firmly that 'there is no sound reason why the citizens of a
state should be concerned with the interests of their fellow citizens, rather

than with the interests of people everywhere'.[7] This raises the issue of why all humans matter, and Singer complicates the issue by showing equal concern for animals, as being also sentient creatures. Yet his stress on the concern of citizens raises the moral issue more fairly than by simply leaving it to decisions by government. The latter should not in a democratic society pursue an agenda that is not shared by its citizens, and even prompted by them.

A generalized concern for all, however, does run up against a major obstacle. In the development of modern states, the principle of non-interference in the affairs of other states has been made sacrosanct. The United Nations' pursuit of 'decolonization' after its foundation was conducted with the belief in a people's right to self-determination. The argument was that it was better for a state to be sovereign and independent than governed by a foreign power. Even if a colonial government might govern better, and avoid the corruption and civil wars which sometimes followed independence, that appeared totally beside the point. Political autonomy was of absolute importance. Yet this is not a utilitarian argument of the kind being put forward by Singer. Even if a benevolent paternalism might do more good than could be achieved by independence, it was still regarded as wrong. It was better to be governed badly by one's own people than well by an imperial power. Colonialism might, on the other hand, have produced consistently bad consequences, and independence good ones. Yet these issues were not usually argued. Imperialism was thought to be bad for what it was, not for what it did or did not do.

With ideas of sovereignty and national independence so deeply engrained in people's assumptions about international relations, there is the question of how countries, with the best of moral intentions, are entitled to interfere with the internal workings of another country, even if it is to feed the hungry, or ensure basic human rights. The latter task, in particular, could pose a direct threat to a government in power. How far should a government, or an alliance, even for avowed humanitarian reasons, ignore or put aside questions of sovereignty? Dangerous political precedents can be created, but the basic issue is a moral one.

Singer is in no doubt how to decide this kind of question. He claims that 'there is only one standard, that it is right to do what will have the best consequences'.[8] This classic utilitarian principle enables Singer to adopt his universalist approach. He will not give any priority to one people rather than another, nor respect sovereignty as an end in itself. The sole criterion will be what is beneficial. He says unequivocally: 'A global ethic should not

stop at, or give great significance to, national boundaries.'[9] He stresses the
point by saying that 'national sovereignty has no *intrinsic* moral weight'. Yet
the idea of universal need, coupled with a universal responsibility, can bring
us all to moral paralysis. When confronted with the suffering of the world,
where can we hope to start? This question must confront governments as
well as individuals. The idea of a division of responsibility at least means that
we each understand our particular role and its obligations. It makes sense to
recognize that a government has specific responsibilities to its own citizens,
just as individuals have obligations to families. It will be in a good position to
recognize particular needs, and to offer appropriate help. This is not,
however, because its citizens matter more than those elsewhere. Human
needs are not defined by national boundaries. What does vary, however, is
an immediate responsibility for meeting them.

This may seem like a charter for individuals and governments alike to
ignore the suffering of the wider world. Impartiality is an absolute requirement in ethics for many moral philosophers. Humans do not vary in
importance because of their remoteness. Singer is typical of many who
draw large political and moral conclusions from our membership of what
seems a global community. He suggests that we should develop 'the ethical
foundations of the coming era of a single world community'.[10] We should
thus, he considers, constitute, or strengthen, political institutions for global
decision-making, in such a way that they are more responsible to those they
effect. He says: 'This line of thought leads in the direction of a world
community with its own directly elected legislature, perhaps slowly evolving
on the lines of the European Union.'[11] It is remarkable how a moral
argument for a universal concern for all humanity becomes so quickly a
political one about world institutions. Even if it were accepted that we all
have an equal responsibility for everyone, there is still a question as to
whether this cannot be met by the actions of nations as such, perhaps acting
in cooperation. Singer believes that global responsibilities need global institutions. Yet the reference to the European Union illustrates the difficulties.
That Union has a constant struggle not to appear remote and bureaucratic
in the eyes of individual citizens. New loyalties cannot be created instantan-
eously, especially if it means replacing old ones.

The vision of a rationally constructed world order, set to provide 'eternal
peace', is at odds with a different vision, which stresses tradition. Political
structures will not survive if they cannot engage people's most fundamental
loyalties. Politics always needs an underlying moral commitment, which
itself gains strength from basic impulses in human nature. Yet it is a mistake

to oppose reason and tradition, as the Enlightenment tried to do. No human can put aside all constraints, and design a perfect society from scratch. We all carry with us our history and our presuppositions. In addition, we always take our human nature with us. Rational blueprints that fail to take into account the impulses of ordinary humans, good and bad, are liable to destroy themselves in the end. Major revolutions, like those of France and Russia, have started off with great hopes, but, partly because of their attempted repudiation of traditional loyalties, were themselves soon sources of suffering.

Blueprints for world government often involve political solutions to moral problems. They will encounter political difficulties, and it is a fair assumption that they will not succeed unless they can engage the sympathies and loyalties of diverse peoples across the world. Yet the suggestion for world government comes from a commitment to universal reason, and to the idea of a moral code embracing everyone. There is a tension between the idea of a common humanity and that of diverse traditions. Some conclude that recognizing the importance of tradition must involve a postmodernist rejection of universal reason. Yet that is not the basic issue here. Why should a moral commitment to the well-being of everyone lead inexorably to a commitment to global political structures? Many feel that such structures can undermine local traditions. Yet they may still see the importance of a vision of global moral responsibility. Once again morality and politics should not be conflated. Moral claims can be true without needing political structures to implement them. In turn, the existence of such political structures does not guarantee a morally acceptable outcome.

Global Politics

There is a misplaced urge to put morality in concrete. Law and politics may need a moral context if they are to function properly, but morality can never be wholly codified through legal and political structures. Morality is never constituted by convention, or political agreement, and this holds at the international level, as well as more local ones. Singer's universalism, when transmuted into global institutions, represents just another way of turning morality into politics. Judgements about global moral claims inexorably lead him, it seems, to a global politics. We certainly all live in one world. We do not, as the relativist would have us believe, live in different ones, constructed by our society or tradition. Yet the question remains why universal moral claims, arising out of the objectivity of morality, must be reflected in the organization of our political life on this planet. Do ethical beliefs always need to be given substance through institutional structures? The recurring threat is that morality is changed into politics, that questions about truth become changed into a search for agreement and compromise.

One answer to the challenge for a justification for a global politics is that national governments are always going to give priority to their own citizens. Indeed, as we have seen, that is their responsibility. There may then appear to be a case for a world authority whose responsibility is to everyone. This presupposes that national sovereignty will be ignored if it is a matter of meeting needs, particularly of a humanitarian kind. There will be no point in having a world body if it cannot intervene to help, whether or not a local government agrees. Such intervention may be necessary precisely because the tyranny, or corruption, of the local government is the main problem. When human rights are being trampled on, surely international action would be crucial. Yet what one set of people would see as a moral policy, others would view as a typically imperialist imposition of power from outside.

A problem in translating ethical claims into political structures, and then into action, is that it assumes the exercise of a pure, dispassionate reason in everyone's interest. Yet having a world government to implement universal moral principles for the good of all encounters the same problem as Plato's philosopher-kings, or guardians, in his *Republic*. They were assumed to be incorruptible, because they possessed knowledge of the Good. Human beings, however, are not like that. There can never be a guarantee that power and responsibility will always be used wisely. Even if rulers and world governments are totally well intentioned, they can and will make mistakes. They will not have perfect information, and even if they did, their judgement can be faulty. Global governments will make global mistakes, and the results could be far-reaching.

Apart from fallibility, there is also the question of moral corruption. Power can be deliberately misused. Just as there was no one to guard the guardians in the *Republic*, there will be a real question about the moral integrity of those governing the world. One reason why morality can never be identified with politics in any form is that moral claims have to be implemented by politicians, who are subject to all the temptations and personal vanities that the rest of us are. Can we be sure that those governing a world community can be trusted? The answer is that we cannot be, any more than we can expect that members of a national legislature are always going to be paragons of virtue.

At international level the temptations and opportunities for corruption may be even greater, and there will be fewer checks than at national level. The power at the disposal of a global body may be vast, and by definition not subject to any countervailing power. Nation states can challenge each other, and a rogue state be restrained. The 'global community' will have a monopoly of power if it is to achieve anything. Can it be trusted to implement justice? It is in much the same position as Plato's guardians, but there is not as much reason to suppose it will be governed by moral considerations. The guardians had been educated so as to obtain knowledge of the Good and to act in the interests of all. If we can be sceptical that they would do so, we may have more doubts about the implementation of international justice. Individuals may be corrupted, but the whole process will also be likely to be still subject to the vagaries of politics, and to rivalry between nations. Whatever the political arrangements, there will still be local loyalties.

A map in one of the lobbies of the United Nations building in New York celebrates the success of the process of decolonization. The remaining colonies are, for the most part, small islands round the world. Yet the same map does not even acknowledge the existence of Tibet. It has simply been included as a part of China. Is that a judgement based on considerations of justice, or does it merely reflect the power of one nation? International agencies are always liable to reflect the realities of political power, and be imperfect instruments for applying moral standards. It is wrong to follow Peter Singer, and assume that there must be a close relationship between political institutions and ethical claims. Whenever morality is enshrined in human institutions, it is liable to be corrupted.

Does this invalidate morality, or suggest it can never be effective? Some would dismiss claims to an objective morality as hypocrisy, when they see people and institutions failing to live up to their professed standards. Yet even revulsion at moral failure, and moral weakness, has its source in a view of how things ought to be. The very accusation of hypocrisy is rooted in a view of the world that suggests that sincerity and consistency are good, and that a failure to practise what you preach is morally shabby. It too appeals to a moral order.

There will always be a tension between human nature as it ought to be, and human nature as it so often is. Any moral outlook which fails to take into account the real potential for human greed and selfishness is not only naive but dangerous. Granting excessive power to people, or to institutions, in the belief that it will be always exercised properly is an example of this. Any political system, global or local, has to take into account the possibilities for the abuse of power and corruption. The accountability of a government to those governed is obviously an important check, but even there one has to be wary. If what electors believe about a government is important, there must be checks on them being systematically misled. A free press will be one factor, but we always have to rely on the integrity of those in government to be honest about what they are doing. Institutions on a global level combine a dangerous mixture of remoteness from electors and a concentration of power. Yet they will be manipulated not only for personal advantage, but for that of particular nations. International power struggles will not vanish merely because there are institutions for global decision-making. The danger will always be that they will become the vehicle for such struggles.

Morality in International Relations

Much modern rhetoric about human rights presupposes the existence of objective moral standards. Morality, however, does not need a political expression to have a universal application. The fact that institutions can be judged morally defective suggests that they must be judged against something beyond themselves. The alternative is a relativism. Criticism of those who wish to appeal to a morality beyond our shared institutions, and conventions, can take many forms. It can occur in the field of international relations, where those who think that the interests of a state are paramount will naturally resist any superior authority. Others will be distrustful of the metaphysical character of objective standards, or 'values', that seem detached from all contexts. Sometimes the two thoughts coalesce. One writer on ethics in an international context says:

> The problem of ethics and international relations has to be one of reflection and criticism *within* our present practices and institutions, and not one of constructing some brave new world based on blueprints conceived from outside of present politics and law, regardless of whether such a standpoint is conceived as that of God, of the ideal observer, of the felicific calculus, or of the good will itself.[12]

This attacks the idea of any rational reflection on morality, and indeed explicitly makes morality a matter of politics. 'Context-free criteria' and 'idealized assumptions' are to be ruled out. Instead we are to operate within a specific political context, eschewing anything abstract, and denying ultimate foundations for morality. This is a recipe for variations in institutions, with no way of deciding between them. The same author explicitly attacks all attempts 'to define an Archimedean point of view outside of our practices and experiences'.[13] There is, he thinks, nowhere to stand where we can obtain a detached and impartial view of anything. This is a common theme in modern philosophy, and quickly leads to the postmodernist view that we cannot detach ourselves from the restriction of context, time and place. Everything then has the status of conventional, rule-governed behaviour, like rules of the road. This, as we have often seen, is far from a proper understanding of morality. Yet such conventions are good examples of context-driven actions, rooted in the fact of human institutions.

When this kind of view is applied in international relations, the consequence is that moral judgements will only be made from an institutional background, and in particular from the standpoint of a state and its conceptions of its interests. The dismissal of a context-free rationality means that the idea of any judgements being made at a global level must be derided. There could be no way of stepping beyond all existing institutions. It is perhaps not surprising that once Kant's idea of a universal rationality is dismissed, his postmodernist critics would also see little basis for a cosmopolitan, let alone rational, search for global peace.

A school of so-called 'realism' in international relations encourages the single-minded pursuit of national interest. It is often thought, even without the encouragement of postmodernism, that moral considerations do not apply in relations between countries. Hobbes's dictum is often quoted that 'the law of nation, and the law of nature, is the same thing'.[14] Hobbes means us to accept this as the normal way of the world, so that self-defence and security become of absolute importance. One diplomat speaks of the domination of the idea of national interest. He writes: 'According to this dogma [the common catechism of diplomats of nations belonging to all geographical areas, cultures and political orientation], ethics is inevitably subjective, whereas national interest is objective: the former is debatable, the latter is not; the former is abstract, the latter concrete.'[15]

His conclusion is that national interest unites, while ethical preference divides. Yet it is significant how a philosophical doctrine about the subjectivity of morality itself becomes an argument for ignoring moral considerations. This perhaps indicates how important it is to be clear about the objective basis of morality, it if it is to be taken seriously. There is, however, also an assumption that it is always obvious what is in the 'national interest'.

The notion of interest is bound itself to be influenced by moral considerations about what is truly important. We might agree that no state should suffer invasion or military defeat, but, beyond that, things may not be so clear without some moral guidelines. Giving independence to a colonial empire may not appear to be in a nation's interests. Its power will be curbed. From another point of view, however, putting into practice the ideals of democracy and freedom by which a country lived might seem to be very much part of its interests. 'Realism' can involve a particular, and rather narrow, thesis about what constitutes interests. It will tend to concentrate on military and economic advantage, and neglect the importance of spreading ideals. International relations will be seen as mere conflicts of power.

No nation can be so naive as to be oblivious to the importance of power if it is not to become defenceless. Yet thinking that this is all that matters is itself tantamount to a moral decision. It is a paradox that those who wish to opt out of moral decisions, and claim to be operating in an 'objective' and 'value-free' manner, are very often indicating that they are going to behave immorally. Any doctrine exempting the behaviour of nations from moral scrutiny celebrates the fact of power as the most important element in human relations, at least at the collective level. Yet if human beings matter, and if they have rights, it is irrelevant from the moral point of view whether they are made to suffer by individuals, or a collective body, such as a nation.

The idea that the nation-state is beyond morality itself acts as an argument for the importance of power, rather than morality. It amounts to the view that might is right. Indeed, if one assumes that national interests are normally economic, it is easy for international relations to lapse into a form of economic determinism, whereby it is assumed that the behaviour of nations is conditioned by the pursuit of perceived economic interest. Talk of international justice will then be viewed as mere rationalization, cloaking the deliberate pursuit of economic advantage. Unless we affirm the possibility of a moral outlook, nations could be seen as mere puppets on an economic string.

If morality is seen as embedded in institutions, it may appear inapplicable in areas where there are none. That may encourage some to press for the establishment of a world government, so that a global morality could take a concrete form. As we have seen, this carries with it its own problems. Large, global, enterprises are too abstract and remote to meet ordinary human needs and command our loyalties. More local institutions may relate to people better, but could fail to recognize the importance of our fellow human beings in other places. Human nature in fact tugs us in two directions. We are divided into nations, which command our loyalties, but at the same time we should recognize that we all share the same human nature. The dedicated and single-minded pursuit of national interest can forget the claims of that common humanity.

Any moral outlook must bring us back to the global claims of humanity. Yet it is an illusion to think that these can necessarily be met by establishing appropriate institutions. That will always be a separate political question, carrying with it its own difficulties. The Enlightenment trust in reason may encourage a search for world government. A postmodernist distrust in it may stress local loyalties instead. Yet there should not be a choice between being a citizen of the world or of a country. We are all human, and at the same time we all belong somewhere. Morality does not demand the repudiation of special responsibilities, since the very idea of a responsibility is itself deeply moral. Yet it does demand that we extend our concern to every human. Morality can never be reduced to the operation of politics at whatever level. Even global institutions must be subject to its claims and may fall short of its demands. The universality and objectivity of the moral claims upon us can never be totally identified with a global politics, any more than international relations can neglect ethical considerations which transcend the interests of particular nations.

Notes

1 John Rawls, *The Law of Peoples*, Harvard University Press, Cambridge, MA, 1999, p. 79.
2 Immanuel Kant, 'Towards eternal peace', in *Principles of Lawful Politics: Immanuel Kant's Philosophic Draft toward Eternal Peace. A New Faithful Translation with an Introduction, Commentary, and a Postscript 'Hobbism in Kant?'*, ed. Wolfgang Schwarz, Scientia Verlag, Aalen, Germany, 1988, p. 74.
3 Ibid., p. 87.
4 Margaret Thatcher, *Statecraft*, Harper and Collins, London, 2002, p. 263.
5 Ibid., p. 264.
6 Peter Singer, *One World: The Ethics of Globalization*, Yale University Press, New Haven, CT, 2002, p. 20.
7 Ibid.
8 Ibid., p. 139.
9 Ibid., p. 148.
10 Ibid., p. 198.
11 Ibid., p. 199.

12 F. Kratochwil, 'International law as an approach to international ethics', in Jean-Marc Coicaud and Daniel Warner (eds), *Ethics and International Affairs*, United Nations University Press, Tokyo, 2001, p. 18.

13 Ibid., p. 31.

14 Thomas Hobbes, *Leviathan*, Oxford University Press, Oxford, 1996, p. 235.

15 Roberto Toscano, 'The ethics of modern diplomacy', in *Ethics and International Affairs*, p. 49.

one world: a global ethic?

10

Character and principle

The Importance of Character

Morality is not a political matter of negotiating and engineering compromises to suit various pressure groups. It is matter of genuinely discerning what is in the interests of people. We have seen how all human beings have a claim on us, even if we also have particular responsibilities. There are also wider questions about moral issues concerning our treatment of animals, and the natural world as a whole. The objectivity of morality, and any idea of natural law, means that questions about what is right and wrong, or good and bad, cannot be viewed as conventions for a particular society. Similarly, they are not to be left to the tastes of individuals. Morality concerns truth, so that contradictory moral judgements made in the same circumstances cannot both be right. Morality matters, in both private and public life, precisely because we can make judgements which can prove to be terribly mistaken. As long as relativists follow the rules of their own society, they cannot be wrong. Subjectivists will say that morality is a private affair, and it must be left to individuals to make up their own minds. Again there can be no possibility of error.

Morality is not primarily a negative matter, concerning what we wish to condemn. It is above all concerned with what we, and others, ought positively to do. Actions are important, but is that all? Should we also be concerned with the character of agents? There is a difference of emphasis if we ask 'what sort of people should we be?' rather than 'what kinds of actions should we perform?' This becomes an important question in public life, where it is sometimes thought that the way politicians behave in their private life is irrelevant to their performance of their public duties. This makes sense if actions alone matter. If public duties are performed satisfactorily, that may seem to be enough. If 'character', however, is brought into the equation, then someone who is dishonest in one area of life may well be in another. A man who deceives his wife may also be likely to think nothing of deceiving the electorate at large.

Aristotle certainly thought that a 'good' character was important for the conduct of a moral life, and many have followed him over the centuries in placing great emphasis on the acquisition of 'virtue'. Indeed, a moment's reflection will demonstrate that any separation of action from character must be artificial. We may do good by accident, but if we do, our good actions are likely to be sporadic. If we intend to do good, we have to become the kind of people who are ready to act like that. We must, in other words, act well because that is what we mean to do. We must acquire the appropriate character. Aristotle thought that we acquired virtues by exercising them. He claimed that just as 'men become builders by building, and lyre-players by playing the lyre, so too we become just by doing just acts, temperate by doing temperate acts, brave by doing brave acts'.[1] Habit is, he thought, a crucial part of moral education, and there must also be the implication that we cannot divide up our lives into different compartments. We have to have an integrated personality so that some kinds of actions become second nature, whatever the context, whether in our 'private' lives or on the public stage. Aristotle makes the etymological link between the word 'ethics' (itself a Greek word) and the 'ethos', the Greek word for 'habit'.

How relevant are Aristotle's views for modern life? His list of virtues, like courage, owes much to his idea of what was required of a citizen in a Greek city-state. Nevertheless, his emphasis on the importance of acquiring a certain kind of character through habit has a modern resonance. 'Virtue ethics' has undergone a recent renaissance, and is often thought of as an alternative to ethical positions such as those of Kant, stressing duty and principle, and utilitarianism, stressing the centrality of the consequences of action. Utilitarianism appears to focus on results, so that character can only be important in so far as it helps to produce actions with the best consequences. Inevitably, however, motives, and intentions, are going to be secondary to what is actually achieved. Individual 'virtue' could even appear irrelevant. Virtue ethics, by contrast, calls for the development of good character, and entrusts moral decisions to it. A strict adherence to principle might seem to fail to take account of the features of a particular situation. Indeed, Kantian ideas of following principle, no matter what one's personal inclinations, may seem to many to take insufficient account of the importance of the character of individuals. A stress on virtue, on the other hand, considers that central importance lies with the kind of person I am, and not what I happen to accomplish.

One problem with talking about virtues in the Aristotelian sense is that it can appear to divide personality up in an atomistic way. One upholder of 'virtue ethics', Rosalind Hursthouse, concedes that it may be wrong to see virtues, like courage or justice, as 'discrete, isolable character traits'.[2] As she points out, the ranges may overlap, and anyway, 'the same sorts of judgments about goods and evils, benefits and harms, what is worthwhile and what is unimportant, crop up all over the place'. This may go some way to explain why 'virtue' is often seen as homogeneous. We all know that someone can be courageous without being just, but, at root, we often do feel that people's actions reveal the kind of people they are. A man's neglect of his family might be a sign that he may not care too much, either, for other people's interests in his professional life.

'Good Character'

'Integrity' is often prized as a characteristic, suggesting honesty and reliability across the board. The acquisition of 'good character' used to be thought vital in education. Yet despite the impact of virtue ethics, there are those who would query whether all this is as important as many think. Experimental evidence from psychology is adduced to suggest that minor variations in an external situation are crucial, rather than some ingrained predisposition to behave in particular ways. As John Doris puts it, in a book significantly titled *Lack of Character*: 'In very many situations, it looks as though personality is less than robustly determinative of behaviour.'[3]

Various classical experiments show how people can be influenced, in whether they offer help to someone apparently in need, by very minor external considerations. Doris quotes a famous experiment once conducted with students training for the ministry in Princeton Theological Seminary.[4] Subjects had to fill out a questionnaire in one building, and then report to another to give a short verbal presentation. Some were told they were running late, others that they were on time and others that they were early. On their way to the next building each person passed someone slumped in a doorway apparently in distress. The numbers of those stopping to help varied according to the degree of hurry. Only 10 per cent stopped if they were late, while 63 per cent did if they had plenty of time. It seems that a demand for punctuality, in what might have seemed an unimportant test, was enough to make many ignore what could have been serious, in a context that had deliberate echoes of the story of the Good Samaritan. Yet these were the kind of people whose 'character' might be expected to predispose them to help. According to Doris, so-called 'situationists' draw from this, and similar experiments, the conclusion 'not that helping is rare, but that helping is situationally sensitive'.[5] The idea that character traits are important, and can produce reliable patterns of behaviour, is challenged.

External circumstances, rather than the kind of person I am, may often explain action. As Doris puts it, 'a central challenge for any theory of personality is accounting for the remarkable situational variability of behaviour'.[6] Whether, for instance, anyone stops to help someone who has dropped a folder of papers in their path was found in one experiment to correlate markedly with whether they had just found a dime in the return slot of a telephone when making a call. Doris sums this up by saying: 'If greedy Jeff finds the dime, he'll probably help, and if compassionate Nina doesn't, she very likely won't.' How we behave seems to be a matter of luck. We will be more likely to help just because we are momentarily cheerful after a trivial windfall. Morality seems entwined with accidents. The argument is that personality traits have little to do with how people actually behave.

All this could bring on a debilitating moral scepticism. It may be salutary to realize that 'bad' people can behave well, and 'good' people badly. Does this mean that the attribution of moral character is empirically questionable, and therefore morally useless? Is what someone does in one situation no guide at all as to what they will do in another? A radical conclusion could be that moral education is useless if it is intended to produce character traits, which will be expressed in all kinds of situations. We could well even deny that there is a 'self' capable of taking moral responsibility. Too much stress on external situations can lead to a determinist view that we are creatures of circumstance, pulled this way or that by various stimuli in our environment. A classic example is the medieval one of 'Buridan's ass'. A donkey is envisaged as situated between two bails of hay of equal attractiveness (to donkeys). Each exercises an equal pull, and the donkey is left paralysed with indecision between them. As a result, the poor animal dies. The example is implausible even with animals, but people have powers of reasoning, so that they can decide independently of whatever external pressures they may be put under.

Psychological experiments may show how 'virtue' cannot be taken for granted. We may be easily deflected from what we ought to do. The experiment with the theological students depended on a conflict situation being set up, even if of a minor kind. They were being encouraged to hurry. Yet it was only a conflict because the students believed they ought to be punctual, and not let other people down. This made them ignore real need, but it tells us about how people can behave when put under even minor pressure. Clearly if they were to live under a totalitarian regime, we can expect that even many who are apparently of good character may succumb to explicit and implicit threats, by behaving in ways they ought to find morally repugnant. That was certainly a common experience in Europe under the Nazis, and the Communists, when it required considerable inner strength to stand out against those who were prepared to use force and other pressure to make people conform to their wishes.

All this tells us nothing about the underlying morality of a situation, or about the inner conflicts that may be set up. As we shall see, there is plenty of room for guilt, shame and remorse, even when people are induced to do something which they ought not to. A 'good character' may not be a guarantee of perfect behaviour, even by the agent's own standards. Weakness of will has always been recognized by moral philosophers as a major stumbling block in implementing moral principles. Yet there is still a difference between those who have the moral sensitivity to feel remorse, and those who do not. This is no doubt one reason why religion sees confession, whether public or private, as an important element in moral growth. It is not as much a bleak acknowledgment of failure as a necessary component of a future strengthening of character, and a determination to do better in the future.

When, on the other hand, 'character' is devalued as an explanation for behaviour, and we are seen as being manipulated by external situations, it is hard to see how anyone can be morally responsible, or be capable of improvement. Humans can behave badly, whether in the trivial circumstances of a psychological experiment or in the terrible conditions of a concentration camp. That does not mean there is no such thing as character. Aristotle was right, in that the more we are habituated to do certain things, the more we will become the kind of people who will do those things. We may fail, but character development should mean that we can improve. Without the idea of character, the very idea of improvement becomes nonsensical. We (whoever 'we' then are) are going to be merely the creatures of circumstance.

Even the ideas of character and of virtue can have their dangers. Doris claims that it is not an accident 'that the discourse of character often plays against a background of social stratification and elitism'.[7] 'Good character' can become identified with a particular position in society, perhaps with being a 'gentleman', and with such ideas as 'respectability'. A cynic might point to the social stratification of a Greek city-state, in which the citizen body excluded slaves and women, not to mention foreigners. Similarly, a Victorian stress on the building of character may have explained much about the English public school system, but it left vast swathes of the population out of account. However, any stress on individual moral responsibility must show that a position in society is not the point. Even Aristotle saw that, and in referring to those who are well born, or who have power and wealth, he says firmly that 'in truth the good man alone is to be honoured'.[8] Virtue, as expressed in a person's character, is not, and cannot be, linked to social prestige. The two may very well not go together. Indeed, at times, the person of good character may have to risk losing respect and social standing in the pursuit of what is right.

Liberalism and Character

Plato and Aristotle were well aware that moral character is of particular importance for politics. Being in power and using it properly are two different things. Political leaders should certainly be trustworthy, reliable and otherwise of 'good character'. There is, however, a more fundamental issue facing those who want to uphold liberal democracy. Modern political philosophy has all too often wanted to break any connection between politics and morality. Once the protection of individual liberty has been seen as the most important role of government, it may seem as if moral judgements made by the state will undermine the personal autonomy it is attempting to safeguard. Yet if the state is morally neutral, how can it ensure that its citizens are of the kind necessary to uphold liberalism itself? This is crucial, as it is no use supposing that the maintenance of a liberal society comes 'naturally'. Even if it is characteristically able to meet basic human needs better than alternative political arrangements, that does not mean that the respect for individuals it encourages will come easily. Humans seem to be too greedy and grasping, seeking for personal power and advantage, if left without any moral guidance.

In pointing all this out as a problem which liberalism has to face, one writer says: 'Liberalism's dependence on even a modest degree of virtue can be embarrassing because liberalism must restrain itself from taking all the necessary steps to ensure that citizens will develop the virtues necessary to sustain it.'[9] In other words, liberalism faces what the writer terms 'the problem of character'. However much autonomy citizens should have, and whatever their rights, they should not use their autonomy recklessly or abuse their rights. All states need citizens who are responsible, and who respect each other. Their representatives need to govern in ways which uphold liberal principles, and do not undermine them. This all requires not just restraint but a considerable reservoir of virtue if things are not going very quickly to fall apart. A freedom to exploit and manipulate, to deceive and to corrupt, is not going to support individual liberty or equality. It will undermine it. Dishonest politicians, like greedy citizens, can destroy the freedom which gave them their opportunities. This underlines a fact taken for granted by the classic exponents of liberalism: that liberalism needs a moral basis. The assumption of a 'natural' freedom and equality for all depends on a moral vision of the importance of each human being. Berkowitz contends that none of the major exponents of liberalism (and he names in particular Hobbes, Locke, Kant and Mill) 'imagine that politics can achieve its proper goals if those who govern, and those who are governed, lack the appropriate qualities of mind and character'.[10] Politics, even in its most liberal manifestations, cannot be divorced from morality.

This presents a problem for any liberal. Liberal democracy has to expect responsibilities and duties from its citizens. Among the most basic is that they should be willing to vote in elections. Yet apathy even about that is growing in many countries, and there is a general reluctance to engage in even the minimum amount of political life. Political parties find it hard to engage commitment, and it is difficult to find people who are willing to serve on local councils, and even national parliaments. Sometimes politicians can be blamed for producing through their example a general distaste for any political process. A lack of integrity in those governing can alienate those in whose name they do so. The remedy lies not just in the need for a higher standard of conduct in politicians, but in the way children are brought up. They must come to recognize the importance of public service in its various forms, and be willing to participate because of its intrinsic importance, and not just for hope of personal gain and prestige.

Yet this requires the inculcation of a moral outlook, and goes to the heart of what any morality has to be concerned with. As any stress on 'character' and 'virtue' indicates, moral education is necessary to enable children to become good citizens. This is not indoctrination by a totalitarian, or even a paternalist, state. It is actually a precondition for maintaining any respect for individual liberty and worth. Liberals may feel uncomfortable about recommending any specific moral standards, let alone teaching them through public education. Yet if liberalism is left to take its own chances, it may find itself confronted by a rising generation of determined egoists, who care little for any freedom but their own.

Liberalism is in fact always reluctant to support particular institutions or moral traditions. Religion, for instance, will typically be seen as a private matter. Similarly, modern liberalism is reluctant to support not just a particular model of the family but any idea of a family at all. An extreme individualism can cause it to be silent about how people can best relate to each other and live together. This is a moral vision, but without any kind of religious teaching, specific moral education or form of family environment, it is difficult to see how children can be given any moral guidance. Many liberals would consider that that is a good thing, on the grounds that such issues are for personal choice. Yet a liberal society depends on certain virtues, not least those of toleration and respect, if it is to survive through the generations, and it is unclear how any liberal can be sure that these will acquired. The dilemma faced by liberalism is that it can be cherished if it is transmitted through recommendation and education, and yet that process may seem to encroach on the personal autonomy it holds dear.

Absolute autonomy for the individual must be a mirage. It has never existed and could never exist. No one can make a choice in a vacuum. Existentialism sometimes saw moral choice as analogous to the creativity to be expected of an artist facing a blank canvas. Yet this involves an extreme, and anarchic, moral subjectivism. Moral education becomes a contradiction in terms, since morality can only be a series of arbitrary and undirected choices. Once liberalism accepts that its future depends on the character of its citizens, it cannot leave this to complete chance. The kind of people we are, and the kind we become, will help to form the society we inhabit. No country can expect liberal principles to be adhered to for long without an ingrained willingness on the part of its citizens to uphold them. Liberalism may hesitate to make moral recommendations, but it is itself the result of a powerful moral insight into the nature of human beings. Freedom and equality cannot be taken for granted. Most societies through history have failed properly to respect them. Without a citizen body that respects them, liberalism cannot survive. Yet that brings to the fore the character of the citizens, which must be constantly nurtured. It is a paradox that the liberal stress on the importance of the private, and the individual, brings us back to the indispensability of the public. Without public standards, publicly taught, individuals cannot flourish or hope to implement their personal ideals.

'Dirty Hands'

Whatever characteristics are required of citizens, it is often thought that politics is by its nature a dirty game, and that politicians, by the mere fact of engagement with politics, will not be able to keep their hands clean. Sometimes this view grows out of a cynicism that holds that all politicians are only interested in personal advantage and power. Yet it seems that those in power, merely because of the responsibilities that they hold, sometimes have to do things that in private life would be viewed with horror. Decisions about war or peace are obvious examples, in that a prime minister or president has to be prepared to send armies into situations that can result in many deaths. They have, it may be alleged, to countenance torture, assassination and whatever else may appear necessary to protect those who have elected them. Bernard Williams sums up the situation when he writes: 'It is a predictable, and probable, hazard of public life that there will be those situations in which something morally disagreeable is clearly required. . . . To refuse on moral grounds ever to do anything of that sort is more than likely to mean that one cannot seriously pursue even the moral ends of politics.'[11] This is reminiscent of the idea that morality has no place in business and that ethical objections can be brushed aside by the retort 'That's business'. Morality is, it seems, all very well in private life, but it cannot cope with wider complexities. It is similarly alleged that politics cannot be held back by the simplistic certainties of moral claims. Sometimes this may merely be claiming that ends always justify the means. In other words, it is an assertion of a classic utilitarian position, ranged against absolute demands that there are just some things that should never be done. Yet it is only a small step to saying that we should not expect politicians to exemplify any kind of moral character, because morality and politics do not mix. This then becomes an assertion of the place of morality in the private, and not the public, sphere.

Utilitarians can only give a secondary place to moral character. It is only relevant in so far it makes someone choose the action with the best consequences. Setting an example may matter, but as long, say, as a politician is expert in covering up what is really going on, no great harm will be done. In fact, utilitarianism's concentration on consequences can positively encourage deceit and dishonesty by politicians and officials, merely to prevent the bad consequences of some course of action becoming known. Utilitarianism can in some circumstances encourage the framing of someone. Punishing an innocent person can seem attractive if an example has to be made, or there are pressing reasons for wanting to imprison someone. Any bad consequences, such as a lessening of confidence in the system of justice, can be mitigated if it is kept quiet. Utilitarianism accepts that deceit and unfairness could be beneficial on occasion, and hence contribute to the morality of an action. It appears to turn morality upside down, and encourage apparently unscrupulous behaviour in politicians.

Any doctrine which stresses the role of consequences to the exclusion of other considerations will always face the problem that we can only estimate at any given time what the consequences will be in the future, and we will often be proved wrong. Even if we put this major difficulty to one side, some things may still seem to demand action because of the nature of what they are. If one supports a political party, for instance, calculating whether it is worth going out to vote on a wet night may seem besides the point. Loyalty to a party would demand it. In the same way, it could be alleged, we should refrain from other things merely because of what they are. We have already seen that many would see torture in this light.

Yet this will not satisfy many, who would say that, particularly in political life, there are often hard choices. Is it really desirable that people should refuse to get their hands dirty, no matter what the consequences? Can a politician ever properly be allowed to luxuriate in a clear conscience and 'good character', no matter what happens? What, for instance, of a pacifist who refuses to take measures to defend a country in the face of an attack? The absolutist in morality will refuse to break, or modify, a principle, come what may. There is an ethical purity about such a stance that may be admirable, but one does not have to believe that consequences alone matter to wonder how far it is tenable. Does moral strength of character really demand inflexibility?

The problem is that moral dilemmas seem to be a part of the human condition. For a politician trying to govern, countervailing moral considerations may easily pull in opposite directions. Principles can clash. Political life can be challenging, not because it demands the suspension of morality, but because moral considerations may not give a clear-cut answer. This is not because moral principles are internally incoherent. Life can be so complicated that different principles can apply simultaneously and give different conclusions. There is even the possibility that the same principle, such as a duty to preserve life, can pull in opposite directions. We may find we can only preserve one life by killing someone else, as in a hostage situation. This, though, is not because of any inconsistency about the principle. Life can be tough.

Moral Conflict

Character still matters in such situations. Some may be prepared to kill without any compunction. Yet a principle may still apply, even if we cannot always follow it. Those who find themselves confronted with conflicting obligations, when it is only possible to fulfil one, often face a tragic dilemma simply because the unfulfilled obligation will still exist. Many moral philosophers would say that we cannot have an obligation if we cannot meet it. They will say that we only ought to do what we can do. 'Ought' implies 'can'. Yet, to take an ordinary example, if I have promised by mistake to be in two places at once, it is not enough to shrug, and to think that I am let off the hook, because I ought only to keep one appointment, as I cannot keep both. There is still an obligation to the person I have let down. At the very least I should apologize and try to make amends. Regret, and even a measure of guilt, may be appropriate, as they would not be if meeting one obligation simply wiped the other out. Remorse, in various degrees, is not irrational, but may be the mark of a properly moral agent caught in a tragic situation.

The principle of 'ought' implies 'can', championed by Kant, among others, suggests that morality is more susceptible to neat, rational solutions than it is. We have seen that one principle could simultaneously point in opposite directions. Once we bring several principles into play, as when different human rights are claimed, they may well clash. A plurality of principles will always cause complications. That is one reason why many philosophers have tried to construct a monistic understanding of morality, based on one basic principle. Utilitarians have hoped to do this, but even Bentham found himself with two different standards, the pursuit of pleasure and the avoidance of pain. Weighing one against the other is not very easy.

Others might invoke the 'will of God', but this may not help in moral dilemmas, where it may seem that it is the will of God that we preserve life, but, as when a murderer is on the rampage, we can only do that by killing someone. We are immediately back with the same clash, caused not by any incoherence of principle, or any weakness of character, but by the difficulties and complexities of the real world. Life can be messy, and, however hard we strive, there may be no easy way out. This is true in the life of individuals, and it is even more so in dealing with affairs of state.

'Ought' implies 'can' either suggests a world which is better organized than our own, or entails a willingness to let go of some basic moral insights. We may reason that if we have to do one thing, any other moral claims can be repudiated. Yet if we locate the source of moral obligation in the world, and our relations with others, rather than in our own reasoning, we may find all the demands on us impossible to meet. If we regard ourselves as fully autonomous agents, paying no regard to actual facts, it will be easy to devise a set of consistent principles, which can be suitably modified to meet the occasion. Once, though, we see moral claims as being presented to us, and not to be moulded at will to suit our own preferences, consistency may be harder to achieve. An objectivist ethic, answerable to the world, will always find moral conflict more of a problem than a subjectivist one that can allow our moral outlook to be changed to suit ourselves. Moral character is going to be tested much more when it is tested by external circumstances.

The idea of a plurality of principles, or of ends to be pursued, is sometimes dubbed 'pluralism'. In so far as we are talking of plural goods and evils, the word may be appropriate. However, as we have seen before, it can also be used to describe radical differences in morality between people, and liberals become much exercised about the public role of morality in a 'pluralist' society where many disagree deeply about what is important. A plurality of moral ends, recognized by all, is very different from a plurality of divergent moral positions in a society. In the latter case, there may be little agreement about what is to be counted good. There is no argument about weighting or priority, but instead basic clashes about the kind of thing to be pursued in the first place.

There is a sharp distinction to be drawn between situations in which objectively valid principles cannot all be properly implemented, and ones where there is a conflict between different moral visions. The fact that there is a plurality of moral principles does not contradict the possibility that they are all objectively valid. They continue to make claims on us, even if we cannot meet them, it may be held, precisely because they are objectively true. Yet the second notion of pluralism explicitly rejects this idea of objectivity. For example, the pursuit of justice in a society may clash with respect for individual freedom. Even taxing the rich to help the poor involves a trade-off between social justice and the freedom of each person. The demands of freedom and justice are not contradictory and may be intimately connected. Both may appear important, even if both cannot always be given priority. Yet a totalitarian, and aristocratic, society may have little patience with either. The second sense of pluralism would see this not as a rejection of moral truth, but as the stance of a different morality. There would not be a pluralism of competing, but equally valid, moral principles, so much as a pluralism of moralities. Their source lies not in the one world we all inhabit, but in divergent beliefs and stances. There is then nothing beyond the moral attitudes in question which could settle the matter.

The first kind of pluralism accepts that different principles can be compared. They are not ultimately incompatible, even though applying them all can be difficult in some situations. We can find the world exceedingly complex. Mistakes can be made, and, in any case, moral decisions can incur real costs. The second kind of pluralism merges with relativism, and does not recognize the world as in any sense the source of moral obligation. As a corollary, it cannot recognize that there will be real costs and benefits of any kind as a result of our decisions. According to it, different world-views, and different stances, will set their own standards, and determine with their own presuppositions what is to count as a harm, and what is to appear a benefit. Typically it follows from such a position that there is no human nature against which our morality can be measured. What counts as typically human will depend on the belief-system in question. The whole point of a radical pluralism, like relativism, is to deny that there is anything beyond the moral system against which it could be judged. No morality could then be shown to be true or false, a success or a failure.

Principles which only exist as the product of social agreement or individual choice can easily be revised. They are very far from principles which exert a claim, even when we recognize that we cannot keep to them in a particular situation. Our reactions in such cases of conflict and dilemma are inevitably the product of a feeling that there is an objective order of moral claims, and we are falling short of it, even if we are forced by circumstances to do so. One difference between those with a character attuned to the demands of morality and those without is that the morally sensitive person, whether on the public stage or in private life, will have a greater compunction about going against basic moral principles, or failing to observe such basic human rights as the right to life. When faced with unalterable complexities, and being forced to find a way out of a dilemma, they will be reluctant to do what they consider wrong, and show regret for doing so. We might admire and sympathize with police who have on occasion to shoot and kill to save life, because that may be their duty in carefully defined circumstances. We would be less happy if we found that they were proud, and even exultant, about their tally of victims. We would be more reassured by those who were reluctant to kill, unless it was necessary, and were genuinely sorry for having to do it. Moral character itself matters, even when, as will inevitably happen, we fall short of the principles we accept that we ought to live by.

Notes

1   Aristotle, *Nicomachean Ethics*, Book II, 1.
2   Rosalind Hursthouse, *On Virtue Ethics*, Oxford University Press, Oxford, 1999, p. 131.
3   John Doris, *Lack of Character*, Cambridge University Press, Cambridge, 2002, p. 2.
4   Ibid., p. 33.
5   Ibid., p. 35.
6   Ibid., p. 64.
7   Ibid., p. 168.
8   Aristotle, *Nicomachean Ethics*, Book IV, 3, 1124a.
9   Peter Berkowitz, *Virtue and the Making of Modern Liberalism*, Princeton University Press, Princeton, NJ, 1999, p. 190.
10 Ibid., p. 170.
11 Bernard Williams, 'Politics and moral character', in S. Hampshire (ed.), *Public and Private Morality*, Cambridge University Press, Cambridge, 1978, p. 62.

11

Morality and human nature

Human Dignity

Previous chapters have stressed the importance of being human, and questions arising from our shared human nature. As we have seen, human rights make no sense in the first place if we cannot accept the idea of human nature. Talk of 'human dignity' cannot even begin. Whatever 'our' relations with animals and our more general environment, we have to make up our minds who 'we' are. Yet when we have come across pluralism, and relativism, it has become obvious that the idea of human nature is much contested. For some, such as postmodernists, what 'we' think and indeed who 'we' are depends wholly on where we are. The traditions of a society have moulded us. This itself poses a problem for traditional debates between theists and 'humanists' about the role of God in morality. For example, Jonathan Glover writes: 'If there is to be no external moral law, morality needs to be humanized, to be rooted in human needs and values.'[1] This, though, may be a false dichotomy. Many would feel that the real battle in morality today is between those who believe that there is such a thing as 'humanity', with its specific needs, and its own dignity, and those who break humanity down into many divergent groups, each setting its own standards.

Glover goes on to advocate 'a morality which is deliberately created', suggesting that 'the best hope of this is to work with the grain of human nature'.[2] He is contrasting a humanly constructed morality with an external moral law, no doubt issued arbitrarily from on high by an omnipotent God. Yet those who consider that morality is concerned with human needs, and must take human nature into account, find themselves arguing not with theists, but with atheists who suspect that the very idea of a definite human nature is a result of a theist outlook which saw human beings from a God's-eye point of view. The legacy of thinkers such as Nietzsche involves the denial of any substantive notion of human nature. It cannot then be a standard against which moral decisions must be measured.

This is not to say that there may not be real differences on moral matters between theists and 'humanists', who want to stress the self-sufficiency of human beings. Nevertheless, both agree about the relevance of human nature to morality. On the other hand, the radical pluralism, relativism and nihilism which are all fashionable can have no room for such a notion. Not every moral argument has to become a metaphysical one if it is accepted that human nature is of central importance. People may be able to see truths about what we need as humans, without always questioning why human nature is as it is. Morality has to take account of it, but it may be able to do so in a way that will gain acceptance from people with diverse views as to why humans are as they are. That is another way of saying that we can all recognize the moral importance of natural law, without having to agree as to the source of that law. Evolutionary psychology will look to neo-Darwinism, while other bodies of belief, including theology, will give divergent sources. There may be considerable convergence of understanding about humans, even if it takes place against a backdrop of disagreement.

One problem is how far we must accept human nature as it appears to be. Are the way it is and the way it ought to be necessarily the same? Even here there is more room for agreement than may be thought, in that often we naturally react in ways that cut across human needs. We should therefore learn to control ourselves better. Questions of free will and responsibility come into play, as some, including evolutionary biologists, tend to see human behaviour in severely scientific terms, in terms of cause and effect. Yet unless we can be free, we cannot be morally responsible. Similarly, if we are free to choose, we have to accept that our choices are our responsibility. In a real sense, without freedom there can be no morality.

There are those who would see even in the ideas of freedom and moral responsibility echoes of theology. What, they would say, is responsibility, but the thought that we will be held to account on a Day of Judgement by an omniscient God? The whole idea of responsibility, they would argue, has no grip without a belief in an all-seeing God who can judge who is precisely responsible for what. The idea of free will, it might be said, despite the fact that it appears an integral part of our everyday experience, is simply the corollary of an idea of accountability to a Creator. This all may suggest that morality often carries with it implicit references to a theology now repudiated by many.

Nowhere does this issue become more acute than when we confront the basic problem about why all human beings should matter. That assumption is at the basis of the rhetoric about human rights, and it is not hard to see that religious doctrines may underpin it. What used in pre-feminist days to be called the 'brotherhood of man' is clearly explicitly derived from the idea of the fatherhood of God. We matter to each other, or should do, it might be said, because we matter to God. As humans, we have an inherent dignity, and are set in a natural moral order because that is how God has made the world. Yet the claim that all humans matter, presumably because of our shared humanity, runs into trouble from two opposite directions. Some would deny that humans are more important than many animals. All can suffer. Why then should a fox be of less account than a human being? Indeed, unfavourable comparisons can be drawn between the intelligence, and awareness, of an adult chimpanzee and that of a human infant, particularly if it is born defective in some way.

Others, though, far from extending our moral concern to animals, let alone other parts of our environment, would query whether all humans possess the same dignity and should matter equally to us. Following neo-Darwinism, they would point out that we naturally favour our relatives, who are genetically related to us, through the mechanism of kin selection. We may also cooperate with those who can help us in return, through reciprocal altruism. The problem is then why we should be concerned with those who are unrelated, and who have not the power to give us any aid. Why should we feel any moral obligation to be concerned with those in need at the other end of the earth, who can be no conceivable threat, or help, to us? Neo-Darwinism would contend that we have evolved so as to be morally unresponsive to such situations.

Human rights, as such, can thus be challenged on the grounds that there is nothing special about all humans, or about being human. As we have seen, they cannot exist, too, without some understanding of the objectivity of morals. A major source of a belief in such objectivity is a belief in God. Does it then follow that human rights must be grounded in theistic belief? The problem is that even though there may be anticipated costs and benefits for a large range of people from some course of action, all this is irrelevant if most of them just do not matter to us. The question of why the scope of morality should cover all humanity still presses on us, just as does the problem of why humans have a unique moral status. We may just be prejudiced in favour of humans because we are human ourselves, but that neither justifies the prejudice nor explains why being human, rather than being white, or

English, or male, or whatever, is the most important aspect of people which we will favour.

'Playing God'

Even if we give a moral preference to humans for some reason, it does not follow that animals, and the rest of the natural world, can be exploited for human purposes, with little regard to the future. Can we 'play God' in the sense that we feel that we have the power to use the world to suit our own purposes? The objectivity of a putative natural law may easily extend to the workings of the non-human world. As is worth stressing again, natural law in this sense is normative. It is not like the laws of physics, which describe what does happen. The point of natural law is that it imports ideas of purpose, and tells us what ought to happen if things work as they are supposed to. This is particularly relevant when humans influence their environment. Much of modern human activity has radical effects on the physical world. This does not change the laws of nature, but we are interfering with natural processes in ways we may barely comprehend. Indeed, ecological balances may be upset, and the climate can be changed, even though we may neither realize that this is happening nor intend it. Industrial activity, genetic engineering of crops, even exhaust fumes from cars can all change the nature of the world we live in. Ensuing global warming, including the progressive melting of the Arctic ice-cap, can have profound effects on human lives. In one sense, all that is happening is perfectly natural. It is nature accommodating itself to human activity and reacting to it. Yet we are interfering with the normal course of events in ways that can rebound on human life, and eventually pose great dangers. It is no exaggeration to say that a lack of respect for non-human 'nature' can create a human catastrophe.

We are ourselves a part of the physical world. It may have been designed to work in a particular way, in which case we alter it at our peril. On the other hand, it may simply have evolved by chance through the processes of natural selection. The point is that even if that is so, it is still a complicated mechanism with inbuilt balances. Humans have, for instance, evolved so as to be able to cope with ordinary environmental changes. If we could not do so, we would not have survived this far. Once, though, the system has to cope with new challenges which it has not evolved to deal with, we can expect trouble. To take a real example, one species may be able to cope with a disease, through genetic evolution, and another species may be immune to it. If, however, through interference, the disease jumps a natural barrier, there may be real difficulty.

Whether we begin with theistic premises or neo-Darwinian ones (or, indeed, a combination of the two), the same point holds. Human interference in natural processes, even for the best of intentions, can have far-reaching effects. As with utilitarianism in ethics, we are never in a position to make a proper diagnosis of all the possible costs and benefits that can result. What we are in a position to anticipate, and what actually happens in the real world, may be rather far apart. Human influence will have effects that we may not fully understand, and even worse, that we may not be able to control. Once we have upset an equilibrium in nature, we may not easily be able to repair the damage. Genetically modified crops can have massive effects on the environment (for instance on insect life), and once the pollen is in the air, there is no way its spread can be controlled. This is not say that all human interference with nature is wrong. No one could ever farm if we thought that. It is more a matter of what kind and how radical. A cautious approach is necessary because we have to take seriously human ignorance about the effects of what we do. For this reason, some in this context have talked of the need for a 'precautionary principle', which warns against the possibility of running great, but unknown, risks.

Much the same can be said of the human world, assuming we can separate it from our natural environment. The needs, interests and desires which constitute our common humanity are real enough whether they are God-given, the product of random evolution or, indeed, the result of an intelligently designed evolution. In other words, natural law, even concerning what is good for humans, should be recognized and acted on, regardless of metaphysical belief. The harm we can cause, perhaps without anticipating it, is independent of what we ourselves believe. Hunger and thirst, for example, are not defined by some philosophical doctrine. The conditions in which humans can flourish are very often at the mercy of humans themselves. Whether we mean to or not, our actions can have far reaching effects on how we, and others, live. Indeed, just because it is so difficult to anticipate in a particular situation what the longer-term consequences of our actions can be, this is no doubt a good reason for normally following the guidance of the accumulated wisdom of a moral tradition. Our predecessors very often learnt through bitter experience what can happen, whether they meant it to or not.

Does this mean that appeal to natural law, or something similar, can circumvent moral disputes? It is tempting to think that it somehow provides a neutral arbiter. We only have to point to human harm or benefit, it seems, and we have a means of resolving differences. Certainly such appeals may often transcend some kinds of dispute. For instance, religious believers and humanists might agree on an agenda for helping the needy. Yet things are never going to be that simple. For one thing, there will be disagreement about what constitutes real harm, or good. Humanists and believers will disagree, for instance, about whether mercy killing is a way to deal with suffering. That, in turn, depends on different visions about whether life is a God-given gift or not.

A deeper problem, in which humanists might be ranged with religious believers, is whether we should be concerned with others merely because of our shared humanity. Why do other people matter? Why should we help those who are not related to us, and who could never reciprocate? Religion gives a motivation by appealing to the will and purposes of God. Humanists assume we have an obligation to each other, without giving any metaphysical grounding. The problem is the status of natural law without any such backing. We can say that is just how things are, and that difficulties will be encountered when we go against the grain of nature. People differ as to whether this is an adequate answer to those who do not see why they should help anyone else, if they merely suffer as a result and get no advantage.

Warnings about our natural environment and climate change have a resonance, because we can recognize that we all can become victims of, say, turbulent weather conditions or rampant disease. It is harder to convince some that we all suffer just because of starvation far off in Africa. It may just be a brute fact that all humans are of equal importance, but some will see such a claim as the legacy of a theological doctrine. We each have an intrinsic importance, it may be held, because we matter to God. An unresolved issue is whether, once this belief in God is removed, it becomes harder to talk of the intrinsic dignity and importance of all humans.

Value Pluralism and Objectivity

Views which relate morality to ideas of human nature do not just encounter problems from those who may be chary about an alleged theological bias. Some refuse to accept that we can meaningfully talk of 'human flourishing'.

They will claim that there is no single way in which humans can 'flourish'. William Galston, for instance, claims that 'we are beings whose good is radically underdetermined by our generic human nature'.[3] He thinks that there is a natural diversity among human beings, and says that 'the diversity of human types is part of what exists prior to cultural self-determination'. His point is that we are naturally different, and can then make cultural choices that introduce further differences. He argues for a value pluralism, which holds that there are a variety of goods. There can be no one way of life which is the best. Yet Galston is unwilling to go very far along the road to pluralism. He will have no truck with relativism. Even though he believes that the moral world contains 'plural and conflicting values', they are all objectively good. That is for him the trouble, since we cannot usually choose them all. His stress on the 'wide range of ways in which human beings can flourish'[4] has its limits. We may be able to choose a way of life, but even so not everything can count as flourishing. He gives the following as an example: 'Children who grow up, without attachments to parents and peers, in circumstances of pervasive physical insecurity ... have been harmed, from the standpoint not of some, but rather all viable conceptions of flourishing.'[5]

Even Galston's kind of pluralists have to draw the line somewhere. The real issue is not between them and proponents of natural law, but between relativism and natural law. As we have seen, relativism relates conceptions of flourishing not to the world but to convention. Human nature is seen as socially constructed. Galston, on the other hand, may allow some latitude in what human nature allows. He envisages a wide range of choice of equally valid ways of life. The important point is, however, that he recognizes limits. Not everything can be counted as good for us. The suspicion must be that once one defines the limits more closely, our set of viable options will be drastically reduced. Even if human nature can be compatible with more than one way of life, there are a great many possibilities that will be harmful. No coherent idea of human flourishing can treat lightly the threat of disease and premature death. Practices which make that more likely cannot ever be considered proper choices, unless we are willing to sacrifice ourselves for some greater cause, as when a doctor runs the risk of contracting the very disease he is treating. The point is, though, that it is even then a sacrifice.

Unless we succumb to relativism, and the nihilism it foreshadows, we will have to recognize constraints on our choices. Those constraints may often be neutral between theological and non-theological visions. Smoking kills anyone impartially, whatever their beliefs. We are still left, though, with the question of the equality and intrinsic worth of human beings. How 'natural' is that? Do we need to appeal to a Creator to underwrite it? Atheist creeds from the French Revolution onwards have refused to do so, and that need not be strange from a religious standpoint. If God has created us, and is the source of our reason, we may still be able to use that reason without acknowledging its source. Similarly, if the objectivity of morality owes its origin to conditions created by God, it could be argued that moral matters can be recognized as objectively valid without any appeal to a Creator.

A parallel argument could be made about science. It may be said that the order and intelligibility of the physical world can be traced back to the creative action of God. Nevertheless, although, according to the theist, that creates the conditions under which the practice of empirical science becomes possible, no scientist has to believe in God before recognizing the objective regularity of physical processes. These arguments, however, may be unconvincing to scientists on the one hand, and would-be believers in a moral order on the other. In both cases, they are being told that they do not have to have a religious belief, but that nevertheless the objective state of affairs, which they can see, depends on God. An acceptance of objective truth appears to smuggle in an implicit commitment to theism. It will be no comfort to atheists to realize that this kind of argument is used by postmodernists to suggest that now that theistic belief has been rejected, so must any idea of objective truth, reality, human nature and any other notion which formed a shelter against the gales now blowing of relativism and nihilism. Indeed, according to postmodernism, even atheism, as a claim to objective truth, has to be ruled out.

Some certainly see natural laws as resting unambiguously on religious presuppositions. We have seen how even the United Nations Declaration of Human Rights has a religious resonance. Yet at the same time many proponents of human rights would vehemently deny the relevance of an appeal to religion. However, an American writer, Max Stackhouse, makes the following claim:

> Natural law presupposes that there is a normative, objective moral order in the universe, and that it can be known by unaided (not revealed) human reason. This presumption is, I think, religious on character – profoundly so. Where this religious assumption is not maintained, natural law theory fails, and reason does not lead us to universal moral principles, such as those taken up by human rights concerns.[6]

We are thus brought back to the issue as to whether some notion of an objective moral order has to be theistic. Certainly atheists can, and do, believe in one. The problem is whether, in the end, they are being consistent. Any moral order involves more than the recognition of brute facts about our human nature, and the needs and interests flowing from it. It also takes in the obligations that ensue. It includes not just an understanding of what costs and benefits may arise for humans out of various courses of action. It also involves the realization that all humans matter. Talk of human rights and natural equality acknowledges that facts about human nature are indissolubly linked to correlative obligations. According to this view, facts and values cannot be prised apart in the simplistic manner encouraged by so much moral philosophy.

This is why some, like Stackhouse, may see a religious dimension in talk of the objectivity of morals. When a wedge is driven between the world and our reasons for moral judgement, the 'world' becomes something morally neutral. Moral choices become an outworking of human purposes that seem mysteriously detachable from everything else. Yet we are all ourselves a part of the world. We affect it and 'it' affects us. Yet we have seen earlier how this 'disenchantment' of the world, and the idea that it can somehow be kept separate from the human world in which we indulge our preferences, often seems a central part of modern thinking.

The idea that moral decisions are made because of human purposes and interests, which are not answerable to anything outside themselves, betrays an artificial split between the 'world' (presumably understood as the physical world investigated by science) and the human beings who inhabit it. It is often not clear whether these purposes are those of humanity, of groups or of individuals, and different moral theories opt for a different stress. Yet the point is that human nature cannot be abstracted from our wider environment. We are embedded in it. We react to it and have to deal with it. Our nature is bound up with a wider world, which we may have evolved to be able to deal with. Human choices are not made in a vacuum. They have effects.

Rationality and Freedom

Freedom is an important concept for morality, but there must always be a difference between the freedom to make judgements and act on them, on the one hand, and a wider freedom to decide what will count for us as truth. The latter is no freedom at all. When there is no more reason to choose one thing than another, the result can be paralysis. If nothing is more important than anything else, but it all depends on our choice, it becomes hard to know what to choose. Indeed, there seems little point in choosing. It must be apparent that in those circumstances, whatever we decide will be true for us. All distinction between truth and falsity has been obliterated. We cannot make mistakes or fall into error. Our choices must certainly be free if we are to be responsible, but it is a freedom to be mistaken, even to cause havoc. It is not a freedom to create what is to be important for us from scratch.

Our freedom may be real, but has to be a rational freedom. A freedom where any choice is as good as any other is a freedom where nothing matters. Morality certainly does not. Choice becomes pointless, and belief empty. Without reasons for and against doing something, our actions are simply the end-product of arbitrary causal chains. The role of reason is particularly important in any reference to human nature, and to natural law. Unlike physical laws, which chronicle cause and effect, the whole idea of a natural law in morality is that it is founded on reason. It can be rationally recognized everywhere, like the laws of physics, but, unlike them, it is not enforced through mechanisms in nature. We can choose to act in accordance with it or not.

Our reason should be capable of making clear what helps, and what harms, the interests of societies and of individuals. Even if there may be disagreement about what constitutes a genuine interest, disputes about that can be traced back to different conceptions of the place of human beings in the world, not least about whether we are in a world created by God or not. Morality is, however, never arbitrary, and we should always be able to connect our moral judgements with ideas of human good and harm. One point about stressing natural law, whether or not it can be traced back to the benign intentions of a Creator, is to make it clear that morality is a matter of reason, and not blind choice. The reason for obeying God's commands, if He exists, would be that He is by definition omniscient and perfectly good, and knows what is best for us. Yet it is likely that, if there is a God, He would not give us a set of instructions to be followed blindly. Instead, it might be said, He has given us rationality, so that, within the constraints of our human nature, we can see for ourselves what is good. In that situation, we could always see what is right, independently of any particular revelation. This is why, according to a theistic view of natural law, those who reject the idea of a God who can be revealed can still use their reason. Arguments about what is right according to principles of natural law can then proceed independently of religious belief.

In the eighteenth century, the Anglican Bishop Butler, a noted moral philosopher, poured scorn on the idea that humans naturally pursue their own goodness and happiness, but are indifferent to other people's good and to the good of society. He suggested that there are two rational principles which govern our behaviour, self-love and benevolence. The first is self-regarding and the second other-regarding. One of the problems, according to Butler, is not that people have too much self-love but that they do not have enough. This is because true self-love is not the same as impulsive action, in accord with what I happen to want at some particular moment. It is instead the product of cool, rational reflection about what is genuinely best for me. Many get into trouble precisely because they have not considered their long-term interests. We are liable to forget them just as much as we disregard those of other people. Yet if such interests matter, they matter equally whoever has them. Butler's conclusion is that any comparison of benevolence and self-love makes it as manifest that 'we were made for society, and to promote the happiness of it, as that we were intended to take care of our own life, and health, and private good'.[7]

Butler recognizes that people do not always obey what he considers to be their nature, particularly when they are in pursuit of 'present gratification'. As a result, he says, they 'negligently, nay even knowingly, are the authors and instruments of their own misery and ruin', and 'are as often unjust to themselves as to others'. We have remarked before that we never find it strange that people want what is good for themselves, but we are reluctant to conceive that it is equally natural to want good for others. We may be cynical because of the history of the twentieth century. Yet Butler's point is that the pursuit of one's own good is sometimes as problematic as the pursuit of other people's. He claims that people need more self-love and not less, because following impulses and desires is not usually the way to personal happiness. Prudence has to be as rational as morality. What we see as good in the heat of the moment may be very harmful for us. Too much rich food is a trivial example. It may sometimes seem natural to want something that, given the long view, goes against our real nature. It is therefore rational not to choose it.

Concern for others is, according to Butler, as much a part of our nature as taking proper care of ourselves. That does not mean we always act accordingly. He says: 'Men follow or obey their nature in both these capacities and respects to a certain degree, but not entirely: their actions do not come up to the whole of what their nature leads them to in either of these capacities or respects.'[8] We are often as much the enemies of our own interests as of those of others. The emphasis in contemporary evolutionary psychology on the genetic foundation of natural impulses may encourage the idea that we are in the grip of forces beyond our control. Yet unless it undermines the idea of human rationality completely, it could also draw our attention to the fact that these forces actually are in need of discipline and direction. In our own interest we must not allow them to control us. Reason has to play its proper role in human action. Butler thinks that we have a rational principle of reflection (which he calls our 'conscience'), with which we can approve or disapprove of our actions.

How cynical should we be about all this? It may appear very convenient if we have as much concern for society as for ourselves. It would be important if, as Butler maintains, 'the greatest satisfactions to ourselves depend on our having benevolence in a due degree'.[9] It would be good if we all naturally had a conscience which was more than the product of our upbringing, or of the prejudices of a particular society. Is there, though, any ground for accepting all this? Butler claims that he is looking at human nature as it is, but how can we balance his assertions against the claims of neo-Darwinian biology, stressing the selfishness of each organism, and our own experience of continual human wickedness? Butler's view of human nature may make more sense given a belief in God's intentions for us, and all his claims take place in the context of sermons.

Conclusion

We can underestimate how much we take for granted in human behaviour. The fact that the rhetoric of human rights finds a ready audience may suggest that, at a deep level, people do respond to calls for justice and fairness. They react angrily to abuses of power and to corruption. Treating individuals as if they are of no account in the end produces repugnance, and, in a political context, rebellion. Some might say that this is just an illustration of the spread of Western ideology, but it seems more deeply rooted historically than that. Not only are our needs and interests crucial, but so is our reason. This has always been the case. It may be significant that Bishop Butler was writing in a very different world from ours, in the stratified society of eighteenth-century England. There were very different social conditions before the Industrial Revolution, and before major political upheavals in Europe, the United States and beyond. Yet his account of human nature, and the problems facing it, remains as apposite today as when it was written. We, as humans, can stand back from ourselves, and reflect on what we are doing. That is as much a part of human nature, distinguishing us from animals, as anything. Once the idea of reason is attacked (sometimes, perversely, from a rational standpoint), and made to appear the product of a particular society and time, morality itself will fade away. It becomes indistinguishable from arbitrary convention and fashion.

Morality depends not just on the fact of rationality, but also on the idea of a common humanity, of which reason is one expression. Most obviously, the notion of human rights will collapse without it. As Robert George, the American legal philosopher, puts it: 'Despite all the differences among the greatest minds that ever applied themselves to the fields of ethics and politics, there is one proposition on which those within the natural law tradition agree, namely that human nature is, in significant respects, determinate, unchanging and structured.'[10] Indeed, talk of a natural law has to dissolve without a definite human nature, whether the result of evolution through natural selection or not. In one sense, how it has been produced, and why it is as it is, may perhaps be regarded as secondary to the fact that humans share many characteristics, just because they are human. This is part of an answer to racists, or to anyone who wished to restrict our sympathies to particular groups to the exclusion of others. Even the positive law of a society will appear arbitrary unless it is seen to rest on an enduring natural law, with its appeals to universal justice, equality, responsibilities and rights. Yet that in turn rests on a conception of human nature. Human actions have to be answerable to external standards of what it is for humans to do well or badly, to flourish or to suffer. There is still plenty of room for disagreement, but all disputes have to be measured against our common human nature.

Moral judgements, however, do not just go with, or against, the grain of our human nature. They also spring from it. This is where questions about whether we have any natural sympathies for each other, or can be educated to have them, become important. Morality is far more than a contract under which we help others in so far as they are willing to reciprocate. Animals are often reluctant to continue cooperating with other animals which accept benefits, such as grooming, without returning them. Human society, however, needs a greater moral commitment than that conditional one. The expectation of reciprocity is not the whole story. The very fact that people who dodge taxes or have free rides through not paying a fare elicit the response that 'it is not fair' illustrates that we have underlying principles of justice and fairness, preceding contracts and agreements. They provide the context in which any agreement can take place.

In the same way, the idea of mutual trust has to be fundamental in any society. Otherwise human beings could never work together. Every time we stop to ask the way in a strange town, or are ourselves asked for directions on home ground, the unspoken assumption is always that we will help each other if we can. In any democracy, mutual trust can be the only basis for citizens to associate with each other. That is why, when it breaks down, for whatever reason, the results can be so serious. Demands for accountability, and transparency, are themselves often symptoms of a calamitous lack of trust that no public procedures can ever restore. We may be, by nature, predisposed to trust each other, but this has to be reinforced through example and education. Trust is impossible if people do not learn to be trustworthy.

Many disagree that there is such a thing as human nature. Many deny that, even if there is, it carries any moral weight. Many deny that reason has any role in establishing morality. Yet in the end all of these protests have to face the question of whether morality is any different from mere convention. If it is more than a series of arbitrary agreements, it must be about what is good for humans. This brings us to the question of what it is to be human. A morality linked to human nature will not say that something is good merely because we want it. We have a reason to want it, if it is good for humans. Such goodness holds whether we realize it or not, and is an objective matter. The nature of morality and human nature cannot be finally separated. It is perhaps not surprising that there are major disagreements in the area of morality. They stem from differences in our most fundamental ideas of the nature of the world, and the place of humans in it.

Notes

1   Jonathan Glover, *Humanity*, Cape, London, 1999, p. 406.
2   Ibid., p. 409.
3   William A. Galston, *Liberal Pluralism*, Cambridge University Press, Cambridge, 2002, p. 59.
4   Ibid., p. 18.
5   Ibid., p. 50.
6   Max Stackhouse, *Creeds, Society and Human Rights*, Eerdmans, Grand Rapids, MI, 1984, p. 107.
7   Joseph Butler, *Sermon* 1, 'Upon the Social Nature of Man'.
8   Ibid.
9   Ibid.
10 Robert George, *The Clash of Orthodoxies*, ISI Books, Wilmington, DE, 2002, p. 158.

Glossary

absolutism: the view that moral principles (such as not to kill) hold in every case, without exception.

altruism: serving another's interests, without hope of gain for oneself.

autonomy: the idea that an agent is free, and under no constraint. Often this is extended to the belief that we are not limited by moral principles, imposed from outside.

Cambridge Platonists: name for a group of theologians and philosophers in Cambridge in the middle of the seventeenth century. They combined Platonism and Christianity, but particularly stressed the role of human reason, providing the philosophical background for the rise of modern science, and the subsequent European Enlightenment.

cosmopolitan: someone who views 'citizenship' of the world, and our shared human nature, as more important than loyalty to any particular country.

determinism: the view that every event has a cause, including human beliefs and choices.

egoism: a belief that one can only act in the light of one's own interests, and help others only if it serves one's own purposes.

empiricism: the philosophical doctrine that all human knowledge is derived only from experience. Our minds are 'a blank slate' at birth on which experience writes.

Enlightenment: the European Enlightenment stressed the pre-eminence of human reason and thought, so that everything – including all tradition and religious revelation – must be subject to its testing. The Enlightenment flowered in the eighteenth century and became progressively more atheistic and materialistic, although it could be argued that in the seventeenth century it had grown from religious roots.

ethics: the theoretical reflection on the nature of morality and the explicit spelling out of moral principles.

evolutionary psychology: the contemporary scientific discipline relating animal and human behaviour to genetic influences. As such, it examines the role of genes in the context of evolution through natural selection.

existentialism: a philosophical position, particularly exemplified by the French philosopher Jean-Paul Sartre, which stresses the importance of absolute freedom of choice, and our responsibility in stamping meaning for ourselves on a world which is at root meaningless.

indeterminism: the view that not everything is determined by any prior causes.

individualism: a belief that society must be explained in terms of the choices and actions of individuals. In a moral context, there may also be the implication that individual choices are to be explained in terms of the desires of the agent.

indoctrination: training someone in a particular viewpoint, as opposed to letting them come to their own views.

judicial activism: a name given to the perceived tendency of judges, particularly when dealing with constitutional matters, to interpret the law in new ways, not necessarily acceptable to a legislature, so as to change social policy.

kin selection: a view stemming from a neo-Darwinian position in biology, holding that we are genetically programmed to favour our children and other relatives, according to how closely related they are to us, and thus share our genes.

liberalism: a view, both moral and political, which emphasizes the importance of individual liberty, and wants to minimize interference from the state or any other agency in how we decide to live our lives.

logical positivism: a movement particularly associated with the 'Vienna Circle' meeting in Vienna between the two world wars. It stressed the importance of a scientific conception of the world, together with logic. Meaning was to be understood in terms of scientific verification or logical tautology.

materialism: the doctrine that everything must be explained in terms of 'matter', and that only 'matter' exists. Aimed against any idea of God, spirit or mind, it finds difficulty in defining matter in terms acceptable to modern science. 'Naturalism' and 'physicalism' encapsulate similar views, both giving priority to science (in the latter case physics) in defining the nature of reality.

metaphysics: any global theory about the nature of what exists, and is real. It is to be distinguished from epistemology, which defines how humans can know what exists.

monism: the view that what is real is of only one kind (for example, matter). Distinguished from dualism, which would posit two different kinds of reality, such as mind and matter.

nationalism: a belief in the supreme importance, and value, of one's own nation, possibly to the detriment of other nations. Distinguished from 'patriotism'.

natural law: in its most general sense, equivalent to laws of nature, i.e. descriptions of regularities in the world. In its moral sense, it denotes what ought to happen to help living creatures to flourish as their nature intends them to.

naturalism: most generally, the view that what is real is what can be discovered by the natural sciences. In a moral context, it is the belief that moral categories can be deduced from statements of fact about the world, or otherwise linked to them.

naturalistic fallacy: the allegation that it is logically fallacious to derive statements of 'value' from statements of fact.

neo-Darwinism: the combination of Darwinian ideas of evolution through natural selection with modern theories of genetics.

nepotism: favouring one's own relatives at the expense of those unrelated. Usually used in a derogatory manner, particularly of those in public life who abuse their power in this way.

nihilism: the belief that nothing matters, there are no objective moral standards, and indeed no objective truth about anything.

nomos: the Greek word for 'law' or 'custom', contrasting what is conventional with what is natural.

normative: whatever carries with it an action-guiding force. In other words, 'norms' prescribe what ought to be done, in distinction from what is being done.

objective: in ethics, and other contexts, the word is opposed to what is 'subjective', and denotes what is true, regardless of what people happen to believe.

pacifism: the belief that violence is absolutely wrong, and must never be used whatever the provocation.

paternalism: a belief that one can know what is in other people's interests, and should intervene to obtain it for them, whether they wish that or not. In other words, one is treating them as children.

patriotism: a love of one's own country, and loyalty to it, but not at the expense of other countries. Contrasted with nationalism.

physis: the Greek word for nature (from which we get the word 'physics'). Usually contrasted with what is conventional in human society.

pluralism: the acceptance that there are many different beliefs and practices, not necessarily compatible with one another. This can develop into a positive welcoming of cultural differences, and can become a full-blown relativism.

postmodernism: a reaction to the Enlightenment conception of rationality, assuming that reason had a universal applicability. It holds instead that all reasoning takes place from within the assumptions of a particular tradition or perspective.

pragmatism: the philosophical view, stemming from American thinkers such as William James, C. S. Peirce and John Dewey, that we should not deal in 'useless' abstractions, but concentrate on what makes a difference in human life, or on what works.

reciprocal altruism: a view arising in the study of animal and human behaviour from a neo-Darwinian perspective. The theory is that an agent will only act to help another if there is a prospect of help in return.

relativism: the view that there are different traditions and ways of life, or different moralities, each to be judged only in accordance with its own standards.

rights: claims that an individual can have on other people and agencies, so that they have a moral, or legal, obligation to meet them. When 'human rights' are claimed, the assumption is that we have them, in virtue of our common humanity.

situationalists: those who claim that the morality of an action depends wholly on its particular context.

sociobiology: the biological study of the development of social behaviour in all organisms including humans.

subjective: opposed in this context to 'objective', it suggests that judgements, like tastes, have a validity only for those individuals making them.

teleology: the view that nature, in particular, is imbued with purpose, so that each thing has its own proper function.

universal: something that holds everywhere, and at all times.

utiltitarianism: the doctrine in morality that the rightness and wrongness of acts depend wholly on their consequences (and not on intentions, or the intrinsic character of the act).

value judgements: decisions about what is desirable, which are often thought to be made from a personal point of view, and not to be open to rational discussion.

values: matters of personal choice and preference about what is worth doing and pursuing, and contrasted with 'facts', which science can determine.

virtue ethics: the view that morality should be viewed in terms of the character of agents, rather than, say, through the nature of actions.

Bibliography

Appiah, K. Anthony and Gutmann, Amy (1996) *Color Conscious, The Political Morality of Race*. Princeton, NJ: Princeton University Press.

Aquinas, St Thomas (1963) *Summa Theologica: Collected Works*. London: Blackfriars and Eyre & Spottiswoode.

Aristotle (1941) *Nicomachean Ethics*. In *The Basic Works of Aristotle*, ed. Richard McKeon. New York: Random House.

Aristotle (1941) *Politics*. In *The Basic Works of Aristotle*, ed. Richard McKeon. New York: Random House.

Arkes, Hadley (1986) *First Things*. Princeton, NJ: Princeton University Press.

Arkes, Hadley (2002) *Natural Rights and the Right to Choose*. Cambridge: Cambridge University Press.

Ayer, A. J. (1946) *Language, Truth and Logic*. London: Victor Gollancz.

Berkowitz, Peter (1999) *Virtue and the Making of Modern Liberalism*. Princeton, NJ: Princeton University Press.

Butler, Bishop Joseph (1970) *Fifteen Sermons Preached at the Rolls Chapel: Disseration of the Nature of Virtue*, ed. T. A. Roberts. London: SPCK.

Coicaud, Jean-Marc and Warner, Daniel (2001) *Ethics and International Affairs*. Tokyo: United Nations University Press.

Dershowitz, Alan M. (2002) *Why Terrorism Works: Understanding the Threat, Responding to the Challenge*. New Haven, CT: Yale University Press.

de Waal, Frans (1996) *Good Natured*. Cambridge, MA: Harvard University Press.

de Waal, Frans (2001) *The Ape and the Sushi Master*. London: Penguin Books.

Doris, John (2002) *Lack of Character*. Cambridge: Cambridge University Press.

Galston, William A. (2002) *Liberal Pluralism*. Cambridge: Cambridge University Press.

George, Robert (1999) *In Defense of Natural Law*. New York: Oxford University Press.

George, Robert (2002) *The Clash of Orthodoxies*. Wilmington, DE: ISI Books.

Glover, Jonathan (1999) *Humanity: A Moral History of the Twentieth Century.* London: Cape.

Gratz v. Bollinger (US Supreme Court), 539 US 244, 123 S.Ct 2411, 156 L.Ed. 2d 257 (2003).

Grutter v. Bollinger (US Supreme Court), 539 US 306, 123 S.Ct 2325, 156 L.Ed. 2d 304 (2003).

Hampshire, Stuart (ed.) (1978) *Public and Private Morality.* Cambridge: Cambridge University Press.

Hittinger, Russell (2003) *The First Grace: Rediscovering the Natural Law in a Post-Christian World.* Wilmington, DE: ISI Books.

Hobbes, Thomas (1996) *Leviathan.* Oxford: Oxford University Press.

Hursthouse, Rosalind (1999) *On Virtue Ethics.* Oxford: Oxford University Press.

Ignatieff, Michael (2001) *Human Rights as Politics and Idolatry.* Princeton, NJ: Princeton University Press.

Kant, I. (1988) Towards eternal peace. In Wolfgang Schwarz (ed.), *Principles of Lawful Politics: Immanuel Kant's Philosophic Draft toward Eternal Peace. A New Faithful Translation with an Introduction, Commentary, and a Postscript 'Hobbism in Kant?'.* Aalen, Germany: Scientia Verlag.

Lawrence v. Texas (US Supreme Court), 539 US 123 S.Ct 2472, 2480, 156 L.Ed. 2d 508 (2003).

MacIntyre, A. (ed.) (1965) *Hume's Ethical Writings.* New York: Macmillan.

Murphy, Mark C. (2001) *Natural Law and Practical Rationality.* Cambridge: Cambridge University Press.

Nussbaum Martha C. (ed.) (2002) *For Love of Country?* Boston: Beacon Press.

Rawls, John (1993) *Political Liberalism.* New York: Columbia University Press.

Rawls, John (1999) *The Law of Peoples.* Cambridge, MA: Harvard University Press.

Rorty, Richard (1999) *Philosophy and Social Hope.* London: Penguin Books.

Singer, Peter (1999) *A Darwinian Left: Politics, Evolution and Cooperation.* London: Weidenfeld and Nicolson.

Singer, Peter (2002) *One World: The Ethics of Globalization.* New Haven, CT: Yale University Press.

Stackhouse, Max (1984) *Creeds, Society and Human Rights.* Grand Rapids, MI: Eerdmans.

Taliaferro, C. and Teply, A. (2004) *Cambridge Platonist Spirituality.* New York: Paulist Press.

Thatcher, Margaret (2002) *Statecraft.* London: HarperCollins.

Trigg, Roger (1982) *The Shaping of Man: Philosophical Aspects of Sociobiology.* Oxford: Blackwell.

Trigg, Roger (1993) *Rationality and Science: Can Science Explain Everything?* Oxford: Blackwell.

Trigg, Roger (1998) *Rationality and Religion.* Oxford: Blackwell.

Trigg, Roger (1999) *Ideas of Human Nature,* 2nd edn. Oxford: Blackwell.

Trigg, Roger (2001) *Understanding Social Science,* 2nd edn. Oxford: Blackwell.

Trigg, Roger (2002) *Philosophy Matters.* Oxford: Blackwell.

United Nations (2002) *Multilateral Treaty Framework: An Invitation to Universal Treaty Participation (Johannesburg Summit).* New York: United Nations.

Index